THE CRITICS K

Praise for

I LOVE GOOTIE *and* ROOMMATES

• • •

"Apple spins a nice anecdote and makes Gootie entirely believable."
— *New York Times*

• • •

"An affectionate and touching portrait of a woman."
— *Jerusalem Report*

• • •

"Apple's strong visual memories and eye for details make Rocky and Gootie emerge as real people."
— *Cleveland Plain Dealer*

• • •

"Charming...transcends ethnic and religious boundaries and speaks to those readers who have ever cherished a caring older relative."
— *Columbus Dispatch*

• • •

"Apple has a sharp eye for the revealing detail....With a rare balance of honesty and sentiment, he conveys the humor and the steeliness of Gootie."
— *Dallas Morning News*

more...

"Apple communicates excellently...a book in which the issues of family, assimilation, and memory are addressed in a tender, funny way."
—*Aufbau Newspaper*

. . .

"Charming and often hilarious...a delightful book, sharp, funny, and familiar without being sentimental."
—*Jewish Bulletin*

. . .

"A delight."
—*Houston Post*

. . .

"Uplifting and unforgettable."
—*Jewish Week*

. . .

"In the era of memoirs, Max Apple's *Roommates* stands out. It is gracefully written, painfully sad, and very funny. It is one of those rare books that alter the way you feel and that you wish would never end."
— Tracy Kidder, author of *Among Schoolchildren*

. . .

"A terrific book...moving and satisfying....An enthralling and novelistic tale of family, guilt, and the rules of survival."
—*New York Times Book Review*

"A tender, tough, and totally compelling account."
—*USA Today*

. . .

"A warm, humorous, and ultimately moving portrait of family life and love."
—*Seattle Times & Post-Intelligencer*

. . .

"A heartwarming story of a strong, vibrant, loving intergenerational relationship...enthusiastically recommended."
—*Library Journal*

. . .

"A memoir that is very funny, very sad, and full of the richness of family."
—*Arizona Republic*

. . .

"A delight starting with the front cover...irresistible."
—*Newsday*

. . .

"A portrait of love, determination, family ties, and devotion that crosses generations, *Roommates* did what few books can do—it moved me to tears."
—*Charlotte Observer*

Also by Max Apple

I LOVE GOOTIE

My Grandmother's Story

MAX APPLE

WARNER BOOKS

A Time Warner Company

Author's Note

Some of the names of people in this book have been changed
to protect their privacy.

© 1998 by Yom Tov Sheyni, Inc.
All rights reserved.
Warner Books, Inc., 1271 Avenue of the Americas, New York, NY 10020
Visit our Web site at www.twbookmark.com

 A Time Warner Company

Printed in the United States of America
Originally published in hardcover by Warner Books, Inc.
First Trade Printing: May 2000
10 9 8 7 6 5 4 3 2 1

The Library of Congress has cataloged the hardcover edition as follows:

Apple, Max.
    I love Gootie : my grandmother's story / Max Apple.
        p. cm.
    ISBN 0-446-52074-8
    1. Apple, Max—Family. 2. Apple, Max—Childhood and youth.
3. Authors, American—20th century—Family relationships. 4. Jews—
Michigan—Social life and customs. 5. Grandmothers—Michigan—
Biography. 6. Jewish women—Michigan—Biography.
7. Immigrants—Michigan—Biography. I. Title.
PS3551.P56Z465   1998
813'.54—dc21
    [B]
ISBN 0-446-67597-0 (pbk.)

Cover design by Diane Luger
Cover photograph by Maxine Apple Winer

For my children
Jessica, Sam, Elisheva, and Leah

Acknowledgments

My friend and assistant, Terry Munisteri, reads my handwriting better than I do and has become, at the very least, an honorary citizen of Serei. Her work is indispensable.

I also wish to thank the following people:

David Kaplan and Joel Cohodes for keeping me in touch with Houston.

Rachelle and Terry Doody for their hospitality.

Frances Mayes and Nancy McDermid for helping me with temporary office space in San Francisco.

Thomas Guynes for solving my computer problems.

Larry Kirshbaum for his patience in waiting for this manuscript and for his careful editing.

Sholom Solomon has been a friend to all the characters in this book. His good deeds are exceeded only by his modesty.

I'm grateful to my mother, Bashy, for remembering the most important things.

My wife, Talya Fishman, hasn't been able to teach me to sing, but that is her only failure—and she's still working on it.

Introduction

I had a grandfather who always stole the show. Rocky was five feet tall. He had a striking head of white hair and was as likely to be running as walking. You couldn't miss him, but if you did, you'd hear him. He was pure energy. Quick and slender, handsome in his brown suit and red tie, his cap angled over his forehead, his blue eyes blazing—he was dynamite, and that was as an old man, a very old man. He lived to 106.

Because his span extended a generation or more beyond that of his friends, I became, in the last twenty years of his life, his friend as well as his grandson. At least I tried. We were even campus roommates when he was in his nineties and I was in my twenties. While the peace movement and the Vietnam War occupied the nation, Rocky and I were having our own battles at the University of Michigan.

In 1994 I wrote a book called *Roommates* that told the story of my life with Rocky. I received hundreds of letters, fan mail for my grandpa. To my readers Rocky became a hero. Whenever I gave a public reading people always wanted to know more about him. There were questions as well about one of the minor characters in *Roommates*, Rocky's wife, Gootie.

I hesitated to say a lot about Gootie. She was a private person; she never liked attention. So I had a standard answer, something like "She didn't do anything—she stayed home. She had a stiff leg, which made it hard to get around, and she spoke only Yiddish." I could usually slip into an anecdote about Rocky to avoid saying more. Of course I knew there was more to say, but not everything needs to be said. I had written a very personal book about Rocky, my young wife's tragic disease, and the early years of my children's lives. That seemed like plenty of family information.

About a year after the publication of *Roommates*, I agreed to be interviewed at a meeting of the Houston Yiddish Vinkel (Yiddish Corner), a Yiddish speakers' club. I expected a half dozen old-timers, and I was ready to yell my answers into their hearing aids. Instead I had a big audience. They were not young. At fifty-three I was still one of the kids, but they were lively, they could hear, and they peppered me with questions. Some spoke Yiddish with a Texas drawl, and some had the heavy Russian accents of post–Soviet Union immigrants.

When members of that audience asked me about Rocky's wife, I couldn't stop talking about Gootie. The Yiddish words rolled off my tongue. The interviewer served hot tea, and I felt as if I were little "Mottele" talking to Gootie instead of about her.

It must have been the Yiddish. In her language it seemed easy and natural to talk about her. In English, when I told questioners that my grandma did nothing, it was true—in English. In Yiddish I began to scratch at the richness of that nothing. "Because she did nothing," I said, "she had time to think about everything and to tell stories." I called her a *cachomie*, a wise woman.

In Yiddish I described Gootie as she was. She never wore a skirt, a blouse, or a sweater, owned no makeup or jewelry. Thick cotton stockings covered her legs, and on her feet she wore fleece-lined slippers. Her half dozen dresses ranged from light gray to dark gray. "You would never notice her," I told the audience, "but she would notice everything about you. That was what she did—she observed."

She was born in 1886, married in 1909, and spent the World War I years in Odessa, separated from her husband, who was already in Michigan. In 1923 she arrived in the United States to begin her lifelong exile from Serei, her beloved shtetl. Yet she didn't leave Serei entirely in Lithuania; she imported big chunks into our house. It wasn't that hard to do. Bashy, my mother and her daughter, had been born there, and my father, Sam, just across the border in Poland. My two sisters and I were born in Grand Rapids but raised in Serei; we saw the world through Gootie's eyes. My sisters gravitated toward American life. I was the youngest, and I lingered. I liked to hang out with my grandparents.

At the Yiddish club, I talked about her and our family life for over an hour. I told my wife how much I loved recalling Gootie, and then, the next day, I forgot the whole event. But for a writer, forgetting is sometimes more complicated than remembering. A few months later, as I worked on the novel I was writing, Gootie showed up. Not a vision, not even a voice. She appeared as a kind of daydream, like my fictional characters. But she came loaded with reality. She didn't need my words; she had plenty of her own. I lay down on the floor beside my desk and let myself enjoy this "visit." Maybe I slept; maybe it only felt like sleep. I sat up, laughing to myself. I had recalled an episode from my childhood, an ordinary event, Gootie and I going out to examine one of the wonders of America.

My sisters told us about the moving staircase at Herpolsheimer's Department Store. Gootie thought it was impossible, but my parents verified the existence of such a machine. Rocky said he didn't care whether it existed or not. But Gootie and I were curious. She wondered how fast it moved and whether she would be able to raise her stiff leg high enough to make an attempt. After my sisters reported on the escalator for a second time, Gootie and I decided to make the trip downtown. I might have been five and she sixty, but we had already been a team for a long time. We had an unspoken deal: I would explain America, and she would tell me about Serei.

The escalator came under my domain. We stood on the ground floor and watched the silver steps ascend. Then I tried to explain. Whenever I used the words "electricity" or "motor," Gootie realized that she would never understand. As we looked up at the machine, I didn't understand, either. Both of us were overwhelmed by this thing in the middle of Herpolsheimer's. For a long time we stared at the riders who stepped on and then disappeared from our sight. A constant stream of people rose and then slowly vanished. There was no sound, either.

"Let's go home," Gootie finally said. "This kind of thing isn't for Jews."

I was an American. I knew better. "I'm going for a ride," I said. "It doesn't cost anything."

"*Ah broch,*" she said.

I pulled my hand free of hers and ran toward the escalator. Gootie followed as fast as she could. "Don't go all the way up," she called to me.

I waved to her. I knew she was praying for my safe return. "I'll come back," I yelled, "from the down side."

When I returned from the opposite direction a minute later, Gootie was still standing at the foot of the up escalator, straining to catch a glimpse of me. I tapped her shoulder.

"Thank God," she said.

"It's not dangerous," I said. "It's fun." On the bus ride home she called me "Mr. Columbus, the big shot." But even though she teased me for being smug about my ride, she liked the escalator. She just didn't like it enough to try it. Trying things was not her method. She preferred to watch what she called America.

By "America" she meant not just the country, she meant the epoch. She left Serei to travel to the time of America. Then she spent the rest of her life trying to figure out what that meant.

I often whipped out my sister's copy of *Michigan, My Michigan* to show her exactly where we were on that peninsula surrounded by the Great Lakes. I showed her: "Across from the thumb. Here."

While I tried to place her in western Michigan in the late 1940s, she was doing her own calculations. She tried to understand the differences between here and there. There—were God and the Jews since the beginning, since before there were Jews; here—were America and Jews who said there was no God. There—was Serei, destroyed; here—America, where it was always the Fourth of July or someone's birthday.

As she inspected and dawdled and drank coffee and sneezed and looked out the window at what the goyim were doing, Gootie sorted. The way she picked through rice for rocks and twigs and burnt grains—she sorted through her history and her memory. She made piles. The big piles were from Serei, the little piles from America.

I watched and listened. Just as she observed America, I observed her. I carried my toys to the kitchen so I could play beside her. Later, as a teenager, I often brought my homework into the kitchen to keep her company. She created Serei for me so well that the first novel I wrote took place there. Her village was as familiar to me as Grand Rapids.

Still, I had no intention of writing about her. After the escalator memory I tried to return to my work, but the fictional people were gone. Gootie and her brothers and Rocky and the whole west side of Grand Rapids in the 1940s and 1950s had pushed them aside. Gootie, who spent her days puttering around in our kitchen, began puttering around in my imagination. It was lovely to have her company as I sorted words the way she used to sort beans and lentils. The differences between here and there, her old job, became mine. There was Gootie; here was I—a lot of space and time between, but it was easy to reach her since I traveled by escalator. It took me straight to her, and I wondered as I rode, just as she did, what happens at the top when the stair disappears.

PART I

Chapter 1

Serei was my Troy and Gootie was its Helen, maybe not as beautiful—she had a longish nose, a few hairs on her chin, loose flesh under her arms—but the beauty was in her stories, not her body. Gootie created for herself and for me a bubble, a timeless scene of those village tradesmen and their wives, busy with making a living, celebrating the holidays, and marrying off their children.

By the time I heard her stories the characters she told me about had all been murdered by the Nazis or by their neighbors. Serei was gone forever—maybe that's why Gootie hung on to it. Or maybe she didn't even need such tragic reasons. Maybe the scenes of her childhood and youth stayed with her as they do for most writers. Only Gootie didn't write. She talked.

For her, pen and paper were worthless; memory was the real treasure. For Gootie, an event remembered could be remembered forever and examined in many ways. In the hundreds of hours that she spent creating Serei for me, no event was more exciting than her wedding. Her wedding became my *Iliad*, her journey to America my *Odyssey*.

I knew the events surrounding that wedding as if I'd been there, even better than if I'd been there. In Serei I would have seen the wedding only once; in Michigan, listening to the bride forty years later, I heard the details dozens of times. In slippers and baggy housedress the bride no longer looked like a bride, but that didn't matter. The characters grew old, not the story. I loved the majestic appearance of Rocky, a young man accompanied by an entourage, two rabbis. No groom had ever come to Serei with his own rabbis. Beryl Leib, the bride's father, pointed this out to everyone. "You see who my Gootie is marrying."

Two of Beryl Leib's sons were already in America. Since they left, he hadn't been able to fill all the orders for bread. In his small saloon in a hut next to the bakery, peasants bought vodka by the glass and slices of dark bread. People said that someday there would be running water and plumbing in Serei, as there already was in some neighborhoods of Warsaw and Vilna, but Beryl Leib didn't need running water. He found what he needed, a son-in-law who could bake.

On Gootie's wedding day there was no business in the town square. Tables covered with white cloths made a straight line from the bakery to the wedding canopy, where the bride would soon stand with her mate. The beggars stayed out of the square so they wouldn't offend anyone until the food came out. They crouched near the blacksmith's shop and the study house and wished every passerby well.

"It's like a fair," Beryl Leib said. "Everyone is happy." He wore a high black yarmulke and a long black coat. His sons wore stiff collars and short jackets that buttoned to the middle of their chests. When he walked into the bakery to summon his only daughter, the sight of Gootie confessing her sins moved him to tears.

She had her mother's long thin face and broad shoulders like her brothers. He told his prospective in-law the truth before he sealed the wedding arrangements and the dowry.

"There's nobody like my Gootie," he said. "If she had been a man, I wouldn't have to worry about what will become of me in my old age. She turned the saloon into a real business. When someone walks in, he doesn't walk out without buying something."

His first two daughters died, one at birth, the other a few weeks after. People warned him to name this daughter "Alte," Old One, in order to fool the demons who hid behind the midwife's skirt, ready to snatch a baby's soul and leave the body as hard as old bread. Beryl Leib had decided to call the baby "Old One" until he looked at her; then he couldn't do it. He spat in all four directions to drive away the demons. Then, after he tied a red ribbon to her wrist to protect her from the evil eye, he named her what she was: "Sheyni Gootkie," beautiful and good.

Until she was three months old, he let no strangers see her. And here she was saying *vidui,* the confessional prayer, cleaning the slate of her twenty-two years of all transgressions so she could go to her husband with a heart as pure as her body. Beryl Leib backed out of the bakery without disturbing his daughter. Let everyone wait, he thought. Let her finish talking to God before she comes out to see her husband.

She had seen him before. After their fathers agreed on the match—subject, of course, to her approval—the groom rode his bicycle to Serei. Yagistov was so far away that horses had to rest twice on the way. There were potholes bigger than wheels in the road, and coachmen bargained twice as much before beginning the journey. Along the way there were highwaymen and no inns or taverns.

Her mother was angry at Beryl Leib for going to Yagistov. There were plenty of boys to choose from in Vilna, where anyone could go by coach.

"I don't want a student," Beryl Leib said. "In Vilna I'll find pale boys with weak lungs who can hardly hold up their books."

Less than a week after Beryl Leib returned from Yagistov to announce the match, without warning, the groom arrived.

Rachel Leah ran into the saloon, where her daughter served herring with vodka and black bread to a farmer.

"He's here," she screamed. "I've never seen anything like it."

"Who?" Gootie asked. From her mother's expression she thought it could be Moshiach.

"The bridegroom," her mother said, "your father's folly on top of a wheel."

Gootie hid in the bakery. She was afraid to look at him. From the bakery and the blacksmith shop people surrounded him. The vegetable sellers ran over for a peek. Children left their mother's side. Beryl Leib had no advance warning. There was no table set, no kerchief ready to make the engagement official. The crowd made the dust rise in the street. When she pulled back the cotton drapery that covered the bakery window and looked with one eye, Gootie saw the dust like a cloud over him. There was no bridegroom; she couldn't see him, even with both eyes. Her mother pushed her way through the crowd. She carried fresh rolls and a pitcher of water so he could rinse his fingers before saying a blessing over the bread. The crowd parted. Rachel Leah beheld her prospective son-in-law.

She fainted. The vegetable sellers picked her up. They held slices of onion under her nose and rubbed garlic behind her ears. They dribbled water from the pitcher onto her eyes. When she arose the crowd had already moved with him to the threshold of the bakery. The workers shouted in Lithuanian. Gootie made certain her sleeves were down and her collarbones covered. She ignored her mother sagging among the onions. He had blue eyes and a crisp mustache. He made a joke about her name, a compliment: *"Du Goot tu zei shayn mir gesundt"* ("If you're Good, then everything is all right"). He walked up to the porch where she stood, grateful to God, who had, with all his other duties, taken time to find her a mate.

When his bicycle fell to the ground, the crowd snatched it. They pushed it carefully as if it were a Torah or a statue of the Virgin Mary. No one in Serei had ever seen a bicycle.

"He was this big," Gootie said. "He came up to my chin. My mother said he could have danced under the table."

Rachel Leah raced to find her husband. "What have you done to your only daughter?" she yelled. "You're going to let her marry a wild man on a bicycle?" The crowd, busy with the bicycle, didn't hear; neither did her daughter, staring into the eyes of her betrothed.

He stood on the porch of the bakery, looking at her. What could she do? She looked back. She had no experience. When she looked at other men it was always with her hand open to accept a ruble for bread or vodka. She forgot her mother; he ignored his bicycle. She had never seen anyone like him.

Beryl Leib ran out to greet him. He wiped the flour and bits of dough from his fingers. "Shalom aleichem," he shouted, "welcome to you. May you come in good health and go in good health."

They sat in the house. Beryl Leib brought out a silk kerchief. He looked at the groom and then at his daughter. Each grabbed an end of the silk. "*Mazel tov*," Beryl Leib said. On a chair behind her husband, Rachel Leah wept.

"What kind of a man risks his life to come on a bicycle," she told her husband, "and who comes unannounced like a plague?"

"He's all right," Beryl Leib said. "In Yagistov he works two ovens at once."

"For bread," Rachel Leah said, "you're giving away your daughter."

"I'm not giving away my daughter. I'm bringing in Yerachmiel, the baker I've been waiting for."

For the wedding Beryl Leib ordered from the mill a whole wagon of white flour, the best quality. When he told his son-in-law-to-be, Yerachmiel said, "If you ordered white flour, then I'm coming to make you a dough like you've never seen."

"Before the wedding?" Beryl Leib asked. He didn't know how people did things in Yagistov. In Serei, before the wedding, people took no chances. The groom said he would sleep on the bakery floor, but Beryl Leib didn't want a son-in-law to sleep like a worker from another town. So they put him at Grandfather Shep-sel's house, even though it wasn't a good omen because Shepsel had already buried two wives and in his seventies married a young widow who was now pregnant with the child of his old age.

Yerachmiel packed his white *kitel*, the gown he would be married in, the gown he would wear on Rosh Hashanah and Yom Kippur and, someday, in his casket. It was the very gown he would be wearing when the Messiah came to pull him from the grave back to life and a bakery. He kept it under a crate of apples, a gift from Grandfather Shepsel's orchard. At Shepsel's they served him meat every afternoon. The pregnant young wife treated Yerachmiel like a scholar.

He woke before dawn and baked cakes that Beryl Leib put aside for the wedding. On Friday morning he baked challah for the town's Sabbath and for his own wedding.

On Saturday morning, the day before the wedding, Beryl Leib and his son-in-law-to-be went to the synagogue together, flanked by the two Yagistov rabbis.

After they read from the Torah and sang from the words of the prophets, the people of Serei made a blessing over the Sab-bath loaf. The Yagistov rabbis said nothing. They chewed and they swallowed. The Serei rabbi, who had an hour before called Yerachmiel to the Torah, tasted the bridegroom's challah. It was his custom to tear a chunk of soft bread, salt it, and feel it melt, like soup, behind his tongue. The son-in-law's bread didn't melt. Beryl Leib slapped the rabbi's back. The holy man's face turned red. They laid him across the table and pounded him with open hands and even with fists. His wife, the pious *rebbitsin*, stuck four fingers into his mouth and pulled his tongue. Finally Eliezer, the butcher, grabbed the rabbi by his ankles and held him in the air as if he were a calf. His black robe fell over his face, his pants exposed his pale legs. The most pious men recited psalms, hoping the Lord would hear their prayers and intervene to save the rabbi. The less pious men watched the butcher shake the rabbi up and down, and together the pious and the less pious saved the rabbi from the hard crust of the son-in-law's challah. It fell from between his lips and made a sound on the earth.

"In Yagistov," the groom said, "people use their teeth."

That afternoon the rabbi, still shaken, went to the Torah to thank God for having spared him. At Beryl Leib's house there was gloom. Nobody ate the soup or the chicken. Rachel Leah said over and over, as if it were the chorus of a prayer, "A wagonload of flour, he ruined a wagonload of white flour."

The groom and his entourage went to Grandfather Shepsel's house and stayed there. People who had seen him reported to Beryl Leib that the son-in-law and the two rabbis were going to leave by coach right after the Sabbath. There would be no wedding.

Gootie's brother Joe, still thin after two years in the Russian army, went to Grandfather Shepsel's to talk to the groom. Joe had delayed his emigration to America until after the wedding. He worried that any day soldiers might claim him for the army again, as they had when he was fifteen. He had heard of such instances when one brother had to serve a second time to make up for a brother who was dead or missing.

"I'm leaving for America," he told the groom and the rabbis, "wedding or no wedding. My mother is upset about the wagonload of flour. For our small bakery a wagonload can last six months. Now she says it will last six years. People will be afraid to eat our bread."

"Did you taste the challah?"

Joe nodded. He looked at his future brother-in-law, a small man with reddish brown hair and a well-trimmed mustache.

"I'm going to America," Joe said. "I'm not much of a baker, and I never was."

"You couldn't bake challahs like these, could you?" Yerachmiel asked.

"No, I couldn't," Joe said. He wanted the wedding to proceed. If it didn't, he might feel even more guilty about leaving his parents in order to join his brothers Louie and Leo, who were already in America, trading in cattle and horses.

"If the rabbi can't chew, is it my fault?" the groom asked.

"Not your fault," Joe said, "not anyone's fault."

Throughout the village of Serei people who had bought the son-in-law's challah chewed with extra care. They broke the bread into tiny pieces, and some of the women, fearing for their children, didn't allow the little ones to fulfill the mitzvah of eating challah on the Sabbath.

Joe walked between his father's house and his grandfather's orchard, trying to make peace.

"Send him away," Rachel Leah said. "This is a sign from heaven that there shouldn't be a wedding. The wagonload of flour will be atonement for you," she said to Beryl Leib, "for what you almost did to your daughter."

"There will be a wedding," Beryl Leib said. He went to his father's house to say the evening prayers with his son-in-law. Just before sundown they broke bread together. Beryl Leib used both hands to break the challah. The two rabbis from Yagistov ate, were satisfied, and thanked God. So did Beryl Leib. The next day Gootie married Yerachmiel.

My great-uncle Joe remembered the wedding, though not as well as Gootie. "I was a seventeen-year-old," he told me. "I just wanted to get the hell out of that country." An old man with a fringe of white hair and a potbelly, he still seemed to me a soldier in the czar's army. Whenever I could, I prodded him for details about Serei. I wanted to know if the bride and groom kissed at the wedding.

"My father kissed him," Joe said. "That's the way they did things over there. Yerachmiel put a gold ring on her first finger. The poor people filled their pockets with cinnamon cake and strudel and whatever else they could get their hands on."

"Did they love each other?" I asked.

"Your grandma got married before there was love," Joe said. "So did I.

"Gootie circled him seven times, and my mother kept saying to my father, 'Your only daughter.' I just wanted to get out of there. When Yerachmiel stepped on the glass I was ready to go to the train station in Vilna. But I had to wait while everyone, the goyim, too, carried him on their shoulders. The men danced until it was dark; then they went by wagon to Vishay, down the road, where her cousin Miriam lived and there was an extra room in the house for the newlyweds. I was in the wagon, too. After the driver dropped them off, he took me to the train station and I left forever. Who ever thought there'd be another war with the Japs?"

"Never saw any Japs at all," Joe said. "I tell people that I fought against the Japs before the Americans did, but nobody has ever heard of the Russo-Japanese War. I hadn't heard of it, either. I think the war must have been over before I got to the front. 'He's a Jew,' one of the soldiers said. 'Put him in the warehouse.'

"I gave out uniforms when they had them. Most of the time the officers sold the uniforms and told me to keep my mouth shut. I never saw a Jap until one walked onto a bus once in Muskegon. And when I told him I'd been in the Russo-Japanese War, he told me he was Chinese."

Rocky had a completely different version of the wedding. He left out all the details; he didn't know how to tell a story the way Gootie did. All he told me was that his father had been fooled. Beryl Leib, a farmer and a small-town entrepreneur, came to Yagistov seeking a match for his only daughter. Rocky's father owned a bakery but preferred to spend his time studying Torah.

"My father knew more than anyone in the community," Rocky said, "and Yagistov was a real city, not a one-horse town like Serei. The farmer told my father that he had a big bakery, that three of his sons had gone to America, and there was too much business for him and the one son who stayed behind. He needed a baker for a son-in-law. My father believed him," Rocky said. "My father believed everyone. He didn't know these small-town con men who will tell you anything to marry off their daughters."

"Are you sorry you married her?" I asked.

"Don't bother me with such questions," Rocky said. "In the Torah it says you should be fruitful and multiply. That's all you need to know."

Chapter 2

I never knew exactly what to think about that wagonload of flour in Serei and the hard challah that almost killed a rabbi. In Grand Rapids everyone said that my grampa was a great baker. Nobody called him Yerachmiel; the bakers couldn't pronounce it. "Rocky" had worked at the American Bakery since 1913. I never heard of anyone choking on his bread.

"Just luck," Gootie said. "At any minute he could still kill an innocent person. That's why my mother didn't want him in Serei," she said. "Even after I had two children in three years she still didn't want him.

"'Send him to America,' she told my father. 'It's a big country—he'll get lost there.'

"'God forbid,' Beryl Leib said. 'You don't separate a husband and a wife.' And my father would never have sent him away no matter what he baked. You know who did it? He did. He wanted to go. When didn't he want to run off somewhere? 'I'll go,' he said, 'and after three months I'll send for you and the children.'

"A lot of men were doing that. They went to America, and sometimes they sent for their wives and sometimes you never heard from them again. My father worried that Yerachmiel would forget us. My mother prayed that it would happen. But he didn't even have a chance to keep his word. After he left they started shooting—who knows why—the goyim started in killing each other. In Serei we were fine, but soldiers came and said all the Jews had to go to Odessa so we couldn't help the Germans.

"'What about my business?' my father said. 'My family, my daughter, and her babies?'

"'We'll take care of your business, don't worry,' the soldiers said, 'and in Odessa you'll be surrounded by Jews. Everyone in Odessa is a Jew. You'll be able to pray all you want.'

"My father said no, we wouldn't leave. It helped like a cold bath. 'You can leave with your suitcases or with the clothes on your back,' the soldier said. So we packed. My mother sewed our money into the featherbeds. My father told me not to worry. 'From Odessa you'll go to America as soon as the war is over. How long can they kill each other?'

"They sent us on freight trains. Every few hours they stopped to let us walk around and go to the toilet in the fields. I let a woman hold my baby, my Mottele, and when I got on the train after a stop I saw that she didn't have him. I screamed for the train to stop, and when it didn't I jumped off to go look for him.

"Everyone cried out and pounded on the walls until the conductor stopped. When they found me my leg was broken in two places. Mottele was asleep the whole time in my mother's arms. My father wrapped my leg in rags and in a towel. One of the Russian train workers gave me a stick to help me walk. By the time we got to Odessa my leg looked like two legs. My toes were blue. My brother Eserkey sold his fur coat to pay for a doctor, the biggest doctor in Odessa. 'The soldiers have it worse,' the doctor told me. 'Their legs are blown right off. If you don't get gangrene, maybe we can save yours.'

"I lay in bed all winter. I forgot about going to America, and I couldn't do anything. My mother took care of Bashy and Mot-

20

tele, my father worked for a shoemaker, and Eserkey bought pig hairs and made brushes out of them. We lived on potatoes. A lot of people didn't even have that.

"They didn't stop killing each other. In Odessa people said that even America had entered the war. The doctor saved my leg. He built me an *aparod*, and I walked around with a big piece of leather and steel. I couldn't go far. My mother had a harder time taking care of me than the children. My father still said I'd go to America someday unless Yerachmiel had turned into a pagan and married another woman and told everyone his wife was dead. By then I didn't even care. It wasn't America that I wanted; I wanted to go back to Serei. I wanted everything to be the way it used to be. But a person thinks and God laughs. I got what I wanted.

"The war ended and the czar said we could all go back to our villages. A lot of Jews didn't want to go back. They were already Communists. In Odessa heaven and earth were turned upside-down. The Communists were in the streets fighting with the soldiers, and this was after the war, when everyone said there was peace.

"'Who needs Odessa?' my father said. 'We're going back to Serei.' He tapped one of the featherbeds full of money. 'We don't have to worry,' my father said. 'We'll have enough until we can start the bakery again.'

"But when we got back to Serei and my father tried to use the money, nobody would take it. There was no more Lithuania, no more Lithuanian money. 'We should have burned it in Odessa,' my father said. 'At least it would have helped keep us warm for a few minutes.'"

Her father, Gootie said, was like Moses looking out at the future. He had to decide what to do for his people. "For my parents and Eserkey," Gootie said, "there was no choice. They had no papers to come to America. But I had a husband. If the president knew what kind of a husband, they wouldn't have given us the papers either. All the Americans knew was that he was a citizen. In America if a person is a citizen, it's like being a king anywhere else.

"My father and I walked out to look at our fields. There was nothing. They had even burned my grampa Shepsel's orchards. 'Odessa,' my father said, 'Serei . . . it's all the same now. We've got nothing here and nothing there—but in America you'll be a citizen.'

"I didn't want to leave; the children didn't want to leave. They didn't know they had a father. Bashy was two when he left, and Mottele six months. They didn't remember him. What was there to remember?

"But we had letters. All through the war he wrote letters, and some of them were waiting in Serei. You should have seen the letters—with pictures of the American Bakery and with him all dressed up like a rich man with a gold watch. 'I've got a big house,' he wrote, 'on Lane Avenue.' What did I know about Lane Avenue or anything else in America? All I saw was a picture of a house and a bakery, and in Serei we couldn't even fix the roof. When it rained we all had to crowd into one room. In the pictures I didn't even recognize him.

" 'Take the children,' my father said, 'and go to America.' What a man Beryl Leib was. He never said a bad word about anyone. He still liked Yerachmiel. 'Maybe he learned how to be a better baker in America,' my father said, 'and if he didn't, he'll find another job. Yerachmiel is not lazy. He'll be a good provider.' Even my father could be wrong sometimes. A provider—well, at least he was a citizen. That much was true.

"We started to get letters every week and papers to fill out; we never saw anything like it. We had to go to a letter writer and pay him to do all the writing. My mother couldn't stand it. Bashy and Mottele were like her own children. 'You go,' she said. 'You go to your half-man. Leave the children with me.'

"That I would have never done, but as far as leaving Serei, I was no more anxious to do that than she was for me to leave. My father said I had to go. 'He didn't forget his wife for all these years; she can't forget him,' he said.

"When they started arguing about what to do, my mother put a cold rag on her forehead.

" 'Beryl Leib,' she said, 'how can you send away your only daughter and her two babies? And think who you're sending her to.'

" 'She's going to her husband,' my father said. 'Every wife should go to her husband.'

"One day," Gootie said, "I'd agree with my mother; the next day, with my father. I didn't know what to do. In Serei there was no more bakery; in Russia, no czar. In America there was Yerachmiel and my brothers and a house on Lane Avenue.

"After we sent in all the papers I still didn't know what to do. I decided that I'd make up my mind when the tickets came. One day I'd think Lane Avenue; the next day, Serei.

"It went on like that for weeks, for months—and at the last minute we got a telegram from America that we couldn't come because of my leg. In America everybody has to be able to run around or else they have to be rich to pay other people to run around for them.

"My mother thanked God. She took the children by the hands and danced. 'I haven't been so happy since before the war,' she said. Then we got a new telegram. He convinced the Americans that he was rich enough to have a lame wife.

" 'America wants you,' my father said. 'They don't care if you can run or even if you can walk. You've got something more important than strong legs—you've got a husband.' "

Chapter 3

*G*ootie's brothers came to America before she did, and all three had their own domestic problems. Joe, my other good source of Serei stories, and Louie, her eldest brother, shared a house in Muskegon. Every month Joe came to Grand Rapids with his big ice chest. After Gootie filled it with baked chicken and ice cubes it took two people to carry it to the trunk of his black Ford.

"He lives like a hermit," Gootie told me. "So does Louie."

Louie never married. Whenever I visited him he promised me a bicycle. I wanted one like my grampa had in the wedding story. When it was time, I would use the two-wheeler to visit my own bride. I didn't talk about a bride, not in front of Louie, for whom God hadn't done his duty as a matchmaker. He hadn't done much for Joe, either. His wife, Sarah, spent her days on the couch. "She's got a bad ticker," Joe said. She couldn't even go upstairs or make the car trip to Grand Rapids.

"My poor brothers," Gootie said. What could she do? She

wrapped the chicken parts in waxed paper and poured ice cubes over the top.

"I don't need so much," Joe said. Gootie ignored him. She stuffed in the wings and the livers that she had already broiled.

"If the car gets stuck," she said, "and the ice melts, don't eat. The chicken could be spoiled."

"I wouldn't know the difference," Joe said.

"You'll know when it feels like you've got cholera and you think you'll be dead in a day."

"If I die, I die," he said. "What's the big deal?"

Gootie looked at me. I knew what she meant. Joe's only child, a boy, died in 1925 of a burst appendix. Without anyone to say kaddish for him, Joe felt bitter about this life and the next.

Gootie changed the subject.

"Joe never recovered from the Russian army," she said. "He was a boy when they stole him."

Joe nodded. "That's right, I was only fifteen," he said. "Two big lugs came and put me in a wagon. They had swords and thick leather boots, and they carried pictures of the czar. 'There's a war, son,' they said. I remember it like it was yesterday. One of them grabbed me and I thought, That's it.

" 'The Japanese have got a million soldiers trying to come in to make slaves of us. You want that to happen?'

"I shook my head. My whole body was shaking, too."

"It's true," Gootie said. "That's the way it happened."

"I thought they were customers," Joe said. "Instead, they carted me away like a bag of flour."

"We said *tehillim*," Gootie said. "We never thought we'd see him again."

"I didn't think so, either," Joe said. "I offered them fifty rubles to let me go. It's lucky they didn't say yes because I didn't even have ten rubles. They'd have killed me for sure."

When I listened to Gootie and Joe, I felt as if I had missed everything: the wars, the revolution, the ships to America. In Grand Rapids all we had were the police on weekends when some of our neighbors got drunk.

Before he and Gootie carried the ice chest to his car, Joe drank tea. He kept a sugar cube between his teeth. The hot tea melted sweetness into his mouth. Every few minutes he opened his lips to show me how much sugar was left. When I tried to imitate him he stopped me.

"Don't use so much sugar yet. Wait until you have false teeth," he said. "Get a good set. Don't try to save a buck."

"Don't talk to him about false teeth," Gootie said. "He doesn't even have all of his teeth yet.

"Get your teeth and keep them," she told me. "Don't listen to him about false teeth. Look at mine. They belong on a horse."

When she laughed you could notice the horse teeth. Her eyes watered and she dabbed at them with one of the giant handkerchiefs that she cut from worn sheets. The handkerchief covered her face. When she wasn't laughing she looked her age, except her hands; soft and unlined, they looked younger than my mother's.

Gootie didn't work. "I'm like a *mashgiach*," she said, "a watchman. I make sure everything is done the right way."

She did her checking at night. She checked all the knobs on all the stoves, the locks on the doors. She made certain that no water dripped from the taps, that no meat dishes or pots had been mixed with any milk utensils. If any dishes weren't clean enough, she rewashed them.

A man named Velvel, who limped like Gootie, had been the town watchman in Serei. Not a policeman, he was just an old Jew who made the rounds. When people knew he was there they didn't worry that their throats would be cut while they slept or that the straw in their mattresses would catch fire. Gootie didn't have a town to watch, just a house. She made the rounds. On Friday nights she watched the candles until they went out. In December she looked out the window at the Christmas tree lights in the neighbors' houses, watching for fires.

She loved magazines and newspapers. She marked the pages that had interesting pictures for me to read to her, but by the time I got around to doing so she usually had made up her own scenario, enough to talk herself out of wanting the stainless-steel pot or the pressure cooker or whatever kitchen item had looked good to her.

The kitchen and kitchen furnishings were the center of her worldly concerns. From her spot at the porcelain-topped table she could look into the dining room and living room, and out her window she could see the foot traffic of Fifth Street and Broadway. Bushes surrounded our house for privacy, but Gootie trimmed them herself to keep the hedges low. She wanted to see out.

Before I could read we read the paper together. She spread the *Grand Rapids Press* wide open on the kitchen table and turned to whatever two-page advertisements there were.

We skipped the words and studied the pictures. All the things for sale in America made Gootie happy about my future.

"You'll sell dry goods in your store," she told me, "not junk. You won't have to put pictures in the paper. People will know that you'll only sell them good stuff. You'll start with sheets and blankets and clothes. And who knows, with God's help, maybe someday furniture, too."

One store meant I wouldn't have to worry; two stores meant I'd be rich. I'd contribute money to help orphaned girls raise a dowry. I'd give to the poorhouse and the TB sanitarium.

"For your wedding," she said, "it will be like a holiday. All your customers will come."

In *Life* and *Look* magazines we studied more personal items, the glossy photos of people showing off white teeth and clean hair. I sang for Gootie the lyrics I heard on the radio: "You'll wonder where the yellow went when you brush your teeth with Pepsodent." I told her she could feel dry all day with Arrid, and I urged her to stop using Fels Naptha soap in the tub so she could glorify her hair with Halo shampoo.

"What a country," she said. "Now they make money polishing teeth. When my brothers got their citizenship papers, nobody wanted white teeth; they wanted yellow. They used to pull their teeth and put in gold ones to look like Yankees. Dentists waited outside the citizenship offices. Pretty soon they'll find a way to make the hair that women shave from their legs and arms grow on men's heads. But in your store, stay away from all that. Let them put in any pictures they want. People will always need winter coats and shoes and socks."

I knew more about my stores than my bride. Whenever I asked what the girl would be like, Gootie described no physical qualities.

"She'll be pious and observant," she told me, "and you won't have to worry about your children, and your house will be so clean you can eat off the floor. You'll come from the store and your food will be waiting for you. On Saturday you'll sit next to her father in the synagogue."

I imagined that my wedding would be like Gootie's and that my bride's father would look like Beryl Leib, who, Gootie said, resembled to a tee her brother Joe.

"There's nothing more important than who you marry," Gootie said. "That's why God himself makes the matches. People help. We make sure that the right man meets the right woman; then God takes over. He picks the man and the woman for one another from birth, then he waits until the world brings them together."

"What about people who don't get married?" I asked. What about bachelors like her brother Louie? Why did God neglect them?

"God tries for everyone," she said, "but people are stubborn or they have bad judgment or they're born in an unlucky hour. My brother Louie for sure. Look what he did. He slept in barns for years. He saved money to bring everyone to America . . . and what happened to him? He rotted his insides with wine. If he had a wife, he wouldn't live like a dog with no food in his refrigerator and wine bottles all over.

"Half the Torah," Gootie said, "talks about who got married and how many children they had. It has never been easy to find the right match, not in the old days and not now, but the one destined for you is always there—that's guaranteed. You can't lose hope."

For her brother Louie she did lose hope. We drove to Muskegon to visit him every Sunday. Instead of listening to the Detroit Tigers on the radio my father packed us into our new car, a 1947 Plymouth with a picture of a clipper ship in the middle of the steering wheel.

Gootie was determined to save her brother with food, but no matter how many chickens we brought, he didn't eat. He grew so thin that the extra leather on his belt hung down to the middle of his zipper. His skin turned yellow. He had no handrail, so Gootie had to lean on me for balance as she climbed to his three-room apartment.

"All I need," Louie said, "is a little rest. Then I'll be good as new."

I sometimes helped him lace his ankle-high shoes. I had a motive for my kindness.

"When I get better," Louie told me, "we'll go to the Bridge Street Tire Company and I'll buy you a two-wheel bike, any color you want."

I prayed for him to get better, and I prayed for him to find a bride. I was in second grade when my father picked me up after school in his truck and told me that Louie was dead.

Gootie sat on a stool for a week of mourning. We covered all the mirrors in our house. For a month we didn't listen to the radio or use the Victrola. I couldn't play my favorite record, "Getzel at the Ball Game," but I knew it by heart, so I entertained the mourners, telling them in Yiddish how Getzel the greenhorn went to see "Yankees"; how the crowd yelled, "Kill the ump," and Getzel hid under the chair in fear; how one man with a big stick came out from underground and another one put a mask over his face and squatted behind him. All the time Getzel thought he was attending an outdoor cantorial concert.

While Gootie mourned I worried that I wouldn't meet my destined bride and that I wouldn't get the bicycle Louie had promised me.

After seven days Gootie uncovered the mirrors and arose

from the stool she sat on. "My brother promised you a bicycle," she said, "so you'll get a bicycle." We took the bus to the Bridge Street Tire Company. We had never been to the store, but we knew Sol Levinsky, the owner. His father, Abe, was Rocky's best friend. When Sol saw us looking at bicycles, he didn't come over. He sent a saleswoman.

"Sol Levinsky, pleez, meesez," Gootie said.

"Honey," the saleslady said, "Sol's busy with other customers. What can I show you?"

The saleslady pointed to the hardware and appliances that filled the store—the tires were outside, chained together and guarded by a police dog.

"Sol Levinsky," Gootie repeated. Gootie wore a babushka on her head, like most of the old Polish women. Her dress had a noticeable tear in the sleeve, the sign that she was a mourner.

"His name is Lee," the saleslady said, "Mr. Lee."

I repeated the name for Gootie to make sure she understood what the woman was saying.

"I don't know any Sol Lee," Gootie said. "That's Sol Levinsky. I see him right over there. Sol," she called out in Yiddish, "this woman doesn't know your name."

"We want a bike," I said, "a red one."

"We got lots," the woman said. "Pick the one you want and I'll ring it up."

I pointed to one I had tried. I could just reach the pedals. I balanced myself between two Gibson refrigerators to see if I could ride it.

"That's a beauty," the lady said, "a Roadmaster."

Gootie shook her head. She told me not to make any deals with this woman. We wanted Sol. Following instructions, I told the saleswoman we would wait for the boss.

"He's busy," she said, "and he doesn't really sell the bikes. That's my area."

Gootie shook her head. She told me that Sol would give us a special price. While we waited I looked at mangles and freezer chests, but I didn't let go of the Roadmaster Junior. Sol knew we were there; every few minutes he looked our way, but he didn't wave or come over.

"Let's go to him," Gootie said. I pushed the bike through the rows of appliances. She followed. Sol stood behind the sales counter, reading a catalog.

"Hello, Sol," Gootie said. "This is the first time I'm in your store. Your father told me you're making a fortune."

"English, please," Sol said. He looked at me. "Tell her English. This is a store, a business."

"English," I repeated to Gootie.

"But she can't say much in English," I told Sol.

"Then you talk," Sol said. "You want that bike?"

"Yes," I said.

He looked at the price tag. "Twenty-nine ninety-five."

Gootie understood. "Too much," she said in English.

"All right," Sol said to me, "gimme twenty-five bucks and take it away."

Gootie shook her head. "Too much," she said again.

Sol slammed the catalog on the sales counter. "You want me to give it to you? You think I didn't pay for the bike plus shipping and overhead? Twenty-five in cash," he said. "I don't bargain. I've got a waiting list for the tires and the bikes, the freezers—what I've got sells fast."

I couldn't translate everything, but Gootie seemed to understand. "Mr. Big Shot," she said, "I knew you when you didn't have a handkerchief to wipe your nose. Now you act like a millionaire. You think you're the only one who made a fortune in the black market? Lots of crooks did." She said "black market" in English. "He had tires during the war," Gootie told me, "when nobody else could get them. He should be ashamed of what he did."

Sol's face turned red. He walked away. Everybody in the store looked at us. Gootie took out her kerchief, unknotted it, and started to count her money near the cash register. The saleslady approached again. Gootie covered the money with her hands as if the woman might steal it. She smoothed and flattened the bills.

"Are we going to get the bike?" I asked.

"We'll see," she said. "Wait."

Gootie sat down on a wooden lawn chair displayed near the register. I stood beside her, holding the bike. Through the open front door I could see Sol talking to people about tires.

"This is what happens," Gootie explained to me, "when a person becomes too rich. When you get rich don't start calling yourself 'Mr. Lee.' And what did he do? Nothing—his father told me. He was lucky. He had tires before the war that were worth a dollar, and suddenly they were worth fifty. For this you don't need a brain."

When Sol walked back into his store Gootie spotted him. "Black marketeer," she said. "Gonif."

Sol kicked the wheel of the Roadmaster Junior. "You want a bike?" he said. "Go to Sears and Roebuck. See what kind of a deal you get from them."

"Sears and Roebuck isn't Abe Levinsky's son," Gootie said. "Sears and Roebuck didn't eat in my house before he was a bigshot millionaire."

"Enough," Sol said. "Talk more quietly." He finally switched to Yiddish, too. "How much do you want to pay?"

"Half price," Gootie said.

"All right," Sol said, "take it and get out."

Gootie counted fifteen single dollars into his hand. "If you ever want a refrigerator or a freezer," Sol said, "don't come back. Everything from now on is full price."

He had a thick black mustache and meaty hands. He picked up the bike and carried it outside. He watched us to make sure we were really leaving. We walked home slowly, Gootie dragging her leg at about the speed I could push the bike.

"I don't like Sol," I said.

"Forget about him," she said. "He still made ten dollars."

Chapter 4

*E*very Thursday after supper, Gootie bathed. She liked water that was too hot to step into. Wearing a gray flannel robe and draped in towels, she headed toward the bathroom. I waited in the kitchen, outside the bathroom door.

"Don't go away," she said. "The telephone can wait; the toys can wait." Before she closed the door she took a last look at the kitchen. If she didn't survive, she wanted to make sure there were no dirty dishes for the mourners.

As soon as the door clicked, I went to work: listening was always my job, but during her bath I listened for sounds, not words. I heard her draw a breath as she put her stiff leg into the water first. Then silence until the other leg went in up to the knee. When she sat, I heard the water lap over the top of the tub onto the two towels she had put on the floor to catch the drops. When she sighed I made sure there were no gurgling sounds. She flapped her elbows for descent, and I heard the bar of Ivory soap make its way through her thin gray hair. Her knees made waves. Some-

33

times I heard her blow bubbles when the water reached above her chin; then I became more alert.

There were dangers beyond drowning. "I might faint," she told me, "from the heat or from relaxing too much. If you hear me go under, call for help—Dr. Schnorr, not Dr. Farber. By the time Farber would come they'd be digging my grave."

Gootie took her bath on Thursday night; my other lifeguarding job came on Friday night when I watched Rocky while he ate fish heads. I had to pound his back and feed him chunks of bread when the tiny bones stuck in his throat. Every week he choked at least once. Gootie splashed and worried, but she never went under.

She came out pink with one white rag wrapped around her damp hair and another around her stiff knee. She looked like a fortune-teller. After she painted her toes with Mercurochrome to guard against infection and put on a flannel nightgown, she called for me. My reward was always the same. I could ask anything, and she would tell me. There were no barriers. Before kindergarten Gootie unveiled for me the secrets of this world and the one to come. I asked her what would happen when she died. It was a natural question. She was sixty-five; we both understood that each bath might be her last. She said her intestines were as ragged as our clothesline; her gallbladder made whistling noises. She lived on chicken soup skimmed twice of fat, on Minute rice, lentils, and Sanka coffee. On rainy days her joints swelled; on dry days the bottoms of her feet cracked.

"Don't worry," she said, "when I die I'll be comfortable. God puts you in a place like the Pantlind Hotel downtown—on a good mattress with a featherbed and a pillow. You rest while you wait for Moshiach, the Messiah. You keep in touch with what's going on in this world, too. You know everything, but you can't tell anyone. That's the real problem with being dead."

After the bath Gootie seemed to hover between this world and the next. She rested against the pillow she had carried from Lithuania. Across her body lay down and feathers that had been gifts from her grandmother. And that old woman had them from her mother and she from her mother. Geese that might have flown over Napoleon still did their job.

The bath even loosened Gootie's prejudices. She admitted that gentiles didn't necessarily want to kill animals and drink and fight, but what could they do? They were the descendants of Esau. And we were equally trapped by Jacob, not so perfect himself. He won his blessing by fooling his brother and then his father, so his heirs had to live by cunning. She liked to illustrate the biblical tales with examples I could understand. Esau, the wild hairy young man of Genesis, had an exact counterpart in Grand Rapids.

"Esau ran around with women," Gootie said. "He was like Ben Rosen."

Right before our eyes the ancient problem renewed itself. Gootie's friend Mrs. Rosen called daily but never visited. Her son had studied pharmacy, and his story became an example to me of what could happen to a man.

"Ben was so handsome," Gootie said, "that girls came from far away to buy pills. They weren't sick. They pretended they had coughs and fevers so they could look at him." She told me that Ben Rosen could have married any Jewish girl in Grand Rapids, or he could have gone to a big city, made a single appearance in a synagogue, and walked out with a bride and a dowry.

"Next to Ben Rosen," Gootie said, "other boys looked like they had TB. He had rosy cheeks and curly hair. The angels that came to visit Abraham didn't look any better."

She sometimes stopped to blow her nose or adjust the rag atop her wet hair. During the pause I thought about the fate of Ben Rosen, a better man than I would ever be. With his angelic face and his pharmacy degree, he spurned his mother and the Jewish people.

The handsome druggist hurried after work to wait outside Wurzberg's department store for the salesgirl who dispensed costume jewelry and cheap perfume. Mrs. Rosen called her "Steenkey."

Gootie and I had never seen Steenkey. Ben was also a stranger to us. But what more was there to know? The story of the temptress was in the Torah: there was Esau's wife; there was Delilah; there was Bathsheba—all Steenkeys of their time. Instead of a drugstore and a Jewish wife, Rosen got his Steenkey. I understood the lesson, and when Gootie was in her postbath ease, when neither of us censored anything, I told her about someone even more remarkable than Ben Rosen. I related the story of the holy birth of Jesus as I heard it in kindergarten at Turner School.

She liked it. "Everyone knows about Jesus," she said, "but I never heard them talk about the star in the sky. You didn't have to be such a wise man to wonder why a star is so bright. Anyone would go to look. I would have gone, too, if it wasn't far to walk. But it's not the true story."

She told me her version of Jesus, how he forced his mother to tell him—"Am I a *mamzer* or am I not? Do I have a father?" His mother, the Virgin Mary, was reaching into a barrel when he confronted her. She was afraid he'd throw her in. He was a smart boy, a magician. He could do anything, but the other children teased him. "All right," she said, "I'll tell. You don't have a father."

That's all he needed to hear. He started doing all kinds of wild tricks. He could make milk turn sour by looking at it. He could appear and disappear like a demon; he could fly on a carpet. One day as he was flying over a field, some women threw rocks and cabbages at him. He wasn't bothering anyone; they just didn't like him. They were jealous. He fell off the carpet. They ran over to taunt him, but he was dead. "*Gevalt*," the women screamed. They didn't mean to kill him; they thought a magician like that would just fly off to some other place. Instead they had to carry him back to his poor mother. Because of those women and what they did, the goyim ever since have been killing Jews to get even.

I believed her Jesus story the way I believed everything Gootie told me. Not as facts—I knew she was wrong about facts. She didn't know what electricity was or how anything worked: a phone, a radio, a car—such things she called "American cleverness." They didn't matter. Let other people worry about such things. She had a more important job. She had to think about what God was doing—why he sent thunder and lightning, when rain alone would have been plenty; why he took away the Garden of Eden but still gave us, in our own yard, beautiful snowball flowers that evaporated in the wind and two kinds of roses, and tulips from Holland.

She didn't think about progress and inventions, the things that interested me. She thought about the rainbow that connected us directly to heaven, and she worried that Muskegon and Alma, the cities where her brothers lived, might collapse under the earth like Sodom and Gomorrah. But probably Grand Rapids would survive because we maintained a synagogue and gave charity to the bearded emissaries who arrived once or twice a year to collect for orphanages and study houses in New York.

The second sweat arrived late, long after she came out of the water. When that happened, she removed the turban from her hair and let me dip it into lukewarm water for her forehead. Drafts of cold air were like enemies waiting to get into your lungs and kill you, but we were lucky. We had a furnace. We lived like kings. Every day someone brought fresh blocks of ice for our icebox, and twice a week the Sealtest man placed milk and cream outside our door. In the winter a dump truck backed into our driveway to unload lumps of number two coal down a chute directly into our coal bin.

"But even in America," Gootie said, "where you have everything, where dogs eat and sleep like humans, look what goes on. People die like flies. They sit down to eat and fall onto their food. Women waiting to marry dry up, and men say, 'Who needs a wife? Who needs children? I'd rather drink beer.' Everybody's got money, and everybody wants more."

She stayed up until about two and slept until ten or eleven. She heard us arise and go to school and to work. She enjoyed all the busyness around her, but she wanted no part of it. She sat in the kitchen and looked on. Everything she saw was strange and new but didn't impress her.

"Do you think people now are any smarter than they were in Moses' time?" she asked me. "Or any stranger than Samson or more beautiful than Queen Esther? And do you think there are bigger miracles than the Red Sea opening up or manna falling from the sky?"

Beyond the great examples from the Bible, she had the more modest characters and events from Serei. Rabbis, merchants, Jews, and gentiles, eating, drinking, doing business . . . "the same as in America," she said, "only for less money."

After soaking in her Michigan tub, Gootie floated on stories. When her sweat passed, when the heat of immersion left her body, she got down to business—observing this world, this little family, what she could see out the window and hear from her grandchildren. She kept her eyes and ears open and her mouth closed to strangers. People thought of her as a recluse. The children who came to play with me thought she was a witch because of the way she stared at them. She knew the days of the week, but not the calendar month or the year, probably not even the century. It didn't matter. From Esau and his wife to Ben Rosen and Steenkey, people did the same kinds of things. Gootie explained these things to me far better than any of my grade-school teachers. I would have preferred to stay home with her, but even when I had to go to school I hurried home at three o'clock to sit at the window with her.

We watched the carpenters and woodworkers leave the American Seating Company and the Widdicombe factory. They carried black lunch pails; the sawdust and wood chips of the morning shift were on their caps.

We liked the workers, and if only we hadn't killed Christ, they would have liked us. They bought their bread at the American Bakery. They came in on Saturdays to turn on our electricity. They were glad to take the chickens we couldn't eat because they had two livers or misshapen entrails or internal tumors.

The workers were like us and not like us. They wore caps like my grampa's. Sometimes a Wolski or an Arsulowicz stopped to have a schnapps. Gootie kept a glass under the sink for them so she wouldn't mix it up with ours. They worked at American Seating. Rocky worked at the American Bakery. They put on clean clothes to march to church on Sunday; we walked to the shul on Front Street on Saturday. Everything was American, the factories, the bread, the TV and movies, the language around us—but somehow, not us, not quite. You could see it in our yard.

We had the only yard on the block. The neighbors had dirt studded with broken beer bottles; we had a birdbath, a tiny grape arbor, and a crabapple tree. We had a little American flag that we put out on holidays. We weren't sure which holidays required it, so we put the flag out for all of them. Yet, in our all-American yard, at its very center, surrounded by chicken wire and hovered over by Gootie, sat an island of Eastern Europe, gooseberries and currants. Gootie didn't allow anyone to touch the berries until they were ripe. When there were spring frosts she covered them with bedsheets. She poured the dregs of Coca-Cola into their roots and sometimes mixed Bayer aspirin into the watering can. Nobody else had gooseberries or currants, not even the A&P.

"We grew them in Serei," Gootie told me. "My father used to look over the gooseberries, and if they were more red than green, he'd say it would be a good year."

When it was time to pick them I stayed home from school to help her. I crawled under the currant bushes and picked from the bottom. They were tiny and soft, just right for a child's hand. Gootie waited for my handfuls with her white porcelain bucket. Usually the currants were ready long before the gooseberries. We ate them quickly—in a few days they turned mushy. They were so small that you couldn't taste anything unless you ate a handful.

The gooseberries were firm. Gootie wanted them picked with just the right amount of red to foretell a good year.

"In Serei," she said, "people who had them gave gooseberries as presents. They were too valuable to use in jam."

I never saw her eat a gooseberry. She kept them in a glass bowl on the windowsill—a sign, if you knew how to read it, as clear as the American flag.

Chapter 5

*I*nside the house we lived in Gootie's shtetl; outside we mingled with the gentiles. Gootie tried to keep me inside and usually succeeded, but for big events she couldn't restrain me. I was in our yard, waiting for the queen of the Netherlands, when I had my first run-in with an enemy.

The queen visited western Michigan to see all the Dutch people in Holland, Zeeland, and Grand Rapids. On this trip, the neighbors said, she was going to buy a desk from the Widdicombe factory. I wanted her autograph. I had a little blue album that Philip Allen, the owner of the American Bakery, gave me for my birthday. I had Philip's autograph and Rocky's and the autograph of everyone else who worked at the bakery. I pestered Gootie until even she made a big X in the book. I had a new white page that I saved for the queen of the Netherlands, and I stayed in the yard, watching for her.

While I waited one of the neighborhood regulars passed by on her way to the liquor store. I saw her all the time but had never spoken to her. Since I had the autograph book ready and since the queen still hadn't come for her desk, I decided to use up the blank page.

"Hi, Two-Bit Sophie," I said. "Could I have your autograph?"

Sophie looked more like a man than a woman. She had thin hair and a potbelly. She wore pants and a flannel shirt.

Sophie looked over the hedge, steadied herself, then threw an empty Goebel bottle at me. She missed. I carried the bottle into the house. Gootie was cooking soup, and Rocky had just come home from work at the bakery. He had his shoes off and was lying down on the couch. He slept for a few hours every afternoon because he went to work at three or four in the morning. Noise didn't bother him. I showed him the beer bottle. He pulled up his suspenders and didn't even lace his shoes. He ran out the door.

"Ah broch," Gootie yelled. She tried to keep me from following him, but I slipped through her hands. When Rocky went after someone I didn't want to miss it. He was about seventy when Sophie threw the bottle at me, wiry as any kid in the neighborhood. And he could run as fast.

He caught up to Sophie before she had gone a block. In the summer everyone played outdoors. The kids all saw Rocky running, and they followed. He cornered Sophie in front of the Marvel Surplus Store—where I wasn't allowed to go because Gootie said they sold the clothes that had been taken off the bodies of dead soldiers.

"They sew the holes and they wash everything twice," Gootie said, "but the blood is still there."

Rocky and Sophie yelled at one another in Polish. Sophie's hair fell in greasy strands almost to her shoulders. I knew all about Sophie. She had a few illegitimate children; she drank at the Alamo Bar. Sometimes she worked at one of the furniture factories, but never for long.

Rocky had to stand on his tiptoes to grab her by the shirt collar. Her beer bottles rattled.

"Beat the shit outta her, Rocky," the kids yelled. Nobody liked Sophie. The kids didn't like Rocky, either. He chased them if he saw them throwing stones at passing cars or smoking cigarettes—but when he had bags of stale sweets from the bakery, he put them on the porch for everyone to take.

Sophie blew out her cheeks as if she were chewing tobacco. She spat a wad at the kids who were yelling for her destruction.

Gootie hobbled up behind me. She carried a broom to use as a weapon. "Elp, police," she yelled in her best English. The kids laughed. In Yiddish she yelled to Rocky, "Get away from her. Are you sorry you've got a grandson? Haven't we had enough tragedy?"

Rocky ignored her; he ignored the kids. His hands were at Sophie's throat. She outweighed him by a hundred pounds and was half his age. She moved under the pressure of his hands, side to side like a telephone wire. Gootie hobbled past me to the thick of the battle.

She used the broom on Rocky, not on Sophie. She prodded him with the handle the way she poked at a chicken in our chicken coop to see how fat it was while we waited for a *shochet*, a ritual slaughterer, to come to Grand Rapids and slice the jugular veins of all the chickens we had. Rocky paid no attention. He had his hands on the enemy. Gootie poked him again.

"Leave her alone," Gootie implored him in Yiddish. "All the men she sleeps with will come at night. They'll burn the house down, then they'll go to the bakery to kill you. Leave her alone. Let her carry my tragedy along with her to the beer garden. God himself will punish her. She doesn't even need any more punishment. Look at her."

Rocky and Sophie held on like dancers on the sidewalk. A few adults watched, too, but nobody tried to stop them. Things like this happened. It was like a dog biting the mailman; it just happened every once in a while. Sophie always got into trouble. Rocky was always after somebody. This was nothing to call the police about, not until there was blood. The kids wanted blood. I did, too—not because I had anything against Sophie—I just wanted to see a good fight, to see Rocky use his left the way my father had showed me how to jab, how to keep a hand in an opponent's face. Bashy and Gootie told me to forget about fighting, and my father winked and promised that he'd take me to see the Golden Gloves bouts when I was a little older.

Rocky didn't punch Sophie; he just held on to her shirt, keeping her in place, keeping her from falling down as she rocked side to side and mumbled to him while she gathered great wads of spit for the kids who came close and ran back every time she let loose.

When he let go of her shirt, Sophie stood there, still rocking, not even aware that she could turn around and continue on her way to the liquor store. Gootie held her broom up as a shield and backed away. Rocky walked toward me.

"She said you called her 'Two-Bit Sophie,'" he said. "Did you?"

"Yes," I said, "that's her name."

He took me by the hand. Sophie waited. The kids waited. Gootie wouldn't let go of my other hand. She wanted to save me from the czar's police, Communists, hoodlums, polio, TB, pneumonia, and lice. Rocky had other concerns. He lived for justice. Everything was either right or wrong, mostly wrong. The world was as clear to him as the Ten Commandments and as exact. If I had done Sophie a wrong, it had to be righted.

He pulled me toward Sophie, rocking left to right, clutching her brown bag of empties. She stopped spitting at the kids who were still hoping for a fight.

"Apologize to Sophie," Rocky said in Yiddish; then he repeated it in English loudly enough for everyone to hear. "Tell her you're sorry."

"I'm sorry," I said.

"Louder," Rocky insisted.

"I'm sorry," I yelled.

Gootie made her way back to my side. Her hand trembled on the broomstick. "Meesez," she said, her voice pleading. She tried English but couldn't: "Er eez a keend." She grabbed my head, showed my face to Sophie to prove I was a child.

"I want my bottle back," Sophie said. "It's worth money."

Gootie offered to bring it so she could escort me back to the house and safety.

"I'll get it myself," Sophie said. She walked back toward our house.

Rocky stayed close. "If you ever throw anything at him again," he said, "no matter what he calls you, I'll break your neck."

Gootie led me into her room. "If she comes in here, crawl under the bed," she told me, "and don't come out. I'll yell, 'Help stealers.'"

Sophie took her empty, and Rocky trailed her to the liquor store to make sure she wouldn't throw another at the kids along the block. On her way home there would be no problems. Sophie wouldn't waste a full bottle.

"You were lucky this time," Gootie said. "Don't go outside alone anymore."

For a long time I didn't. Sophie had scared Gootie more than she'd scared me, but I didn't miss too much by staying inside. Our Polish neighbors came in regularly to use our telephone. Gootie was happy to accommodate them. She listened to all their conversations. When they hung up she offered advice on what she had heard. Once she even had to intervene.

Dorothy, a young woman who lived across the street, used the phone two or three times a week, sometimes to call the police when her former husband came over on weekends to drink and beat her, sometimes to call Kutsche's Hardware, which held the mortgage on her house.

Gootie advised divorce. They were only separated. "Why do you need him?" she said. "Don't even let him in the house."

"I keep thinking he'll change," Dorothy said. "I've got the divorce papers, but I can't make myself sign 'em."

They spoke in Polish. Gootie didn't need me to translate, but she wanted me close by for legal terms like "joint property" and "common-law marriage," even though I had no idea what they meant.

For two years Dorothy hesitated over her husband, but when

44

she didn't make her house payments, Kutsche, the mortgage holder, gave her less than two weeks.

Dorothy came over, clutching the legal note. "I'm gone," she sobbed. "I might as well take poison. They're repossessing me."

Gootie sat her at the kitchen table and poured Dorothy some ginger ale from a fresh bottle. Dorothy put her head on the table. "No husband," she sobbed, "now no house."

"When I came to America," Gootie told her, "they took my house, too. I had only been there a month. I had two little children. My crazy husband went out and bought furniture—first they took that away, then the house. We ended up living above the bakery."

"At least you had something," Dorothy said, "a husband, a family. I've got nothing to live for. I might as well kill myself."

Gootie took her seriously. Everyone had a gun. In October and November the men went deer hunting and came home with bucks strapped across the hoods of their cars. The dried blood stayed on until the snow washed it off. You didn't have to drive five miles to shoot rabbits and squirrels. Most of the boys learned to use a .22 before they could write.

"You can't let them put you on the street," Gootie said.

"I've got nowhere else to go," Dorothy said. "I'm gonna take poison."

Rocky had no sympathy. "If she wants to take poison," he said, "let her take poison." He defended the mortgage holder. "If she owes money, she has to pay."

"Look at him," Gootie said. "God himself would have pity on the poor woman, but he's as hardheaded as his mother. She was a hundred years old and blind, and she would stand by the door of their bakery like a guard, touching people to make sure they paid for everything."

Gootie said Dorothy's life was in our hands. The three of us went to Kutsche's Hardware Store on Monroe Avenue to plead Dorothy's case. Kutsche, Dorothy, and Gootie spoke Polish. I was there for moral support and to translate any English that might arise.

Kutsche ran his mortgage business from the mezzanine overlooking his aisles of hardware. He wore a suit. When he spoke to Dorothy he wrung his hands. He looked to me for help. I was on Dorothy's side.

"She'll take poison," I said.

"They all say that," Kutsche answered. "Someday, when you're a grown-up, you'll understand what I'm up against here. They think because I'm from the old country they can get away with anything. I've got bills myself. Look at all this—" He gestured at his hardware store below us. "You think it's free? I pay, too."

"You'll have a bigger store," Gootie told me in Yiddish. Then she and Kutsche sat down to bargain. Gootie ended up with the house. Dorothy got eight hundred dollars and went to Lansing to live with relatives. She got a job at General Motors and sent us Christmas cards until she remarried and moved out of Michigan.

Every month Gootie and I went to Kutsche's to pay twenty dollars on the mortgage she had assumed.

"He's waiting," Gootie said. "If we're a day late, he'll take the house."

"A shack," Rocky said. "It's not even worth painting. It should be condemned."

Gootie put out a FOR RENT sign. We collected thirty dollars a month. "You see," she told me, "we'll make a profit, and we saved Dorothy from poison. This is how you do good business."

Chapter 6

*I*n the basement beside the coal furnace Gootie and I began preparing for my wedding. We opened the burlap bag full of warm bodies. Gootie put each duck across her knees. She pulled the outer feathers and dropped them into an empty pillowcase. I waited until she had cleared enough feathers for my work to begin. The down was my job.

"Your little fingers can do it better than I can," Gootie said. She praised my work. "First we'll make your pillow," she said, "and then we'll start making one for your bride."

I sat on a child-size couch that had one broken leg, too good to throw away but too damaged for upstairs use. It was exactly the right size for a duck and me. Gootie sat on a wooden stool across from me and stopped to rest frequently. I tried to keep the duck's bloody neck over the end of the couch so I wouldn't have to look at it. Plucking from the body didn't bother me since it was for such a good cause.

"Let's make the pillow for my bride first," I told Gootie.

She often repeated my remark. "You don't even know whether you were born from your mother or your father, and already you're thinking about your bride. You're a smart boy. Your bride will have a better pillow than anyone."

Until I moved on to sports I thought about my own wedding a lot. The pillow would be the star of the event. In the basement we had to work fast, pulling the feathers while the duck was still warm.

We didn't have ducks often, only when my father, somewhere in northern Michigan, met a farmer who sold him a few. They lived in the chicken coop behind our house with the chickens that we bought locally at the farmer's market. We waited for the *shochet*, the slaughterer, to arrive. We never knew when he would show up. Once he didn't come for months. We had to give away the chickens—they went crazy in the small coop. They kept us awake at night. When Weiss the butcher telephoned he only had to say, "He's here," and we tied the chickens' legs and brought them to the shed in the back of the butcher shop.

I hated to watch, but I looked anyway.

The *shochet* was not always the same man. We had to wait for whoever would make the trip. Nobody wanted to come to Grand Rapids to kill chickens.

"Who cares about kosher food in Grand Rapids?" Rocky lamented. "Who cares about the shul or the holidays? It's worse here than in Siberia."

The slaughterers came when they had other business to conduct. Usually they could do circumcisions, too, or sometimes they sang at weddings or wrote out divorces or collected for study houses in Detroit or Chicago or even New York; but to come only to slice a few chicken necks at thirty-five cents each didn't pay—not unless there were hundreds of chickens.

When we drank Sanka coffee together, when we plucked feathers or took the bus to the cemetery or worked in the yard or stayed awake during a thunderstorm, Gootie used every opportunity to tell me about Serei. Sometimes the town was in Lithuania, sometimes Poland, or maybe Russia. They were all the same—a governor, a prince, a tax collector, a czar—to the Jews and even to the gentiles in Serei it didn't make any difference what they called the country. People worked on farms and traded the produce among themselves. They rarely went to Vilna, a two-day ride by horse cart.

The houses were huts and Rocky said the roofs were straw, but Gootie denied it. There were no public schools or factories or cars or buses, but Gootie convinced me that Serei had everything.

We sat between the coal bin and the furnace, underneath the only light bulb. The basement was always damp, and in the summer, when we didn't use the furnace, you needed a jacket even if it was hot outdoors. When we finished the ducks Gootie and Bashy, my mother, would disembowel them and lay the flesh on a long wooden board for salting and then soaking. I didn't care about any of that, only the down, my job. The feathers were valuable, too, but the down was gold. Gootie brought two featherbeds with her from Serei when she risked her life to cross the Atlantic. She said she should have never left Serei. Rocky agreed.

"But if I had stayed," she said, "we'd all be dead. Hitler would have killed us." As it was, Gootie said, the trip almost did her in. When she traveled, the world spun. A fast elevator could make her sick, a sudden stop in the car. On the boat ride from Germany to New York she thought they would throw her overboard.

"I vomited all week. The only reason they didn't throw me into the water was the children. They saw two orphans. And I told them what kind of a person their father was and the captain said, 'We can't do this to the children. Yerachmiel will never raise them. He'll put them in the bakery and make them work day and night. They'll be slaves like the Jews were to Pharaoh.'"

I loved to catch her on realistic details.

"How did the captain know what kind of a man Yerachmiel was?"

"I told him."

"While you were dying?"

"Yes, while I was dying. People listen to a dying person. Before you die your soul sits in your mouth. That's why nobody can tell a lie on their deathbed. That's why they could have thrown me into the water—what difference did it make? I was already a dead person, but I was lucky. God had pity on Bashy and Max."

She shook her head in wonder. "He had pity then," she asked aloud, "why not later?"

Gootie didn't trust God, no matter what she said. I knew that. After Max's death she didn't do anything differently. She wouldn't ride in a car on Saturday or turn on a light or do anything that her parents and grandparents wouldn't have done. She obeyed the rules as strictly as Rocky, but she went to the synagogue only on the High Holy Days, just like the modern people who had been born in America.

I pulled the down until my fingers ached, yet there was barely enough of the fluffy white material to see in the bottom of the pillowcase. I thought I'd never get enough material for even one pillow. "Don't worry," Gootie said, "business will be good. Sam will bring lots of ducks back. You've got time. First you'll have a bar mitzvah, then you'll open a store, then you'll get married.

"You'll walk into the synagogue, and her father will come over to you and ask you if you can say *maftir* [chant the long section from the prophets]. You'll smile and say, 'I'll try.' Then you'll go up and sing without a mistake and you'll give a speech and her father will be so proud, he'll almost explode. At the kiddush he'll announce to everyone that right after the wedding he's going to open a new store for you."

When we were plucking during the winter and Rocky came downstairs to add coal to the furnace, he always tried to make us speed up the work.

"I could finish in ten minutes," he said, and I knew he could, but Gootie wouldn't let him near the ducks.

"He'll leave half the down," she said, "and he'll throw in the toenails and the beaks. You can't trust him with anything important."

"Then why did you marry him?" I asked.

When I looked for evidence of their love I didn't find any. Gootie explained why. "In America there are a lot of people with nothing to do, so they thought up love with flowers and heart-shaped candy and honey sweetheart talk. It's like Halloween when kids dress up and make noise. You want to know about love? This is love."

She placed her coffee cup on one side of the table, my cup of cocoa across from it. "This is men, and this is women. Getting them together is no problem; that they can do even without any-one's help. The problem is making sure you have the right one. All the kissing and looking into each other's eyes, all the fancy clothes and the makeup—none of it means a thing. In fact, it gets in the way. Sometimes a person can be fooled by love and miss out on what should have been. I was lucky," she said. "I didn't have to worry. I knew right away that only God could have sent me a man like him.

"Nothing that people do makes any difference. All matches are made in heaven. In heaven the souls recognize one another, but in this world a soul comes down and right away there's con-fusion. That's why there's matchmakers and dances and parties and all the worrying about should I marry this one or that one."

"What if you marry the wrong one?" I asked.

"It's trouble," Gootie said, "right from the start. The bodies may be fine, but the souls know something is wrong. It's like hav-ing indigestion all your life, but some people don't mind. A matchmaker's job is to keep this from happening. There's no job more important because a matchmaker always has to think about the way things are in heaven—a doctor, a lawyer, a businessman, they don't know anything about the upper realm."

Although she talked about matchmaking a lot, I only saw Gootie actively try to arrange one match. It happened when my father met a man at a gas station in Evart, Michigan. There was only a gas station and a post office in Evart, and who would have believed that a Jewish man lived there? It was like finding life in outer space.

My father invited him for Friday night.

Gootie said he was like a hermit, like the people in Odessa who had to live in permanent hiding from the czar's police. The

51

man, Jerome, still had hair. He said that sometimes he drove into Detroit or Chicago and went to a synagogue, but nobody talked to him. He didn't have stylish clothes. There were no stores in Evart; there were no Jews; there weren't even many gentiles.

Gootie decided that she knew the other half of the match: Goldman's daughter. The meeting took place in our dining room. Gootie and I waited in the kitchen and listened.

"He's dressed up, but his hands aren't clean," Gootie whispered. "He's just like the peasants in Serei were." When he took off his hat Gootie said it was a mistake. "Now she can see that his hair is turning gray."

While Jerome, the man from Evart, and Marian, Goldman's daughter, ate sponge cake and sipped tea, Gootie pointed out to me the loneliness of this single man. "What does he come home to?" she said. "To cold soup from a can. He sleeps alone; he works alone. He doesn't know what the inside of a shul looks like. When he dies strangers will spend his money. . . ." She dabbed at her eyes with a cloth. "In Serei this would never have happened. He would have had a house full of children by now—sons in the yeshiva and daughters already looking for husbands. Instead he's here hoping this old horse will want him."

Jerome scanned our dining room and said nothing.

"What's he waiting for?" Gootie whispered. "Does he think someone is going to send in another woman? He waits forty years for one, and when he sees her he loses his tongue."

Marian picked up a porcelain ashtray. It had slots for a cigarette at each end. In the middle a man with a razor chased a baby boy. It said "Yiddish Clipper."

"Cute, isn't it?" Marian Goldman said.

Jerome nodded. Marian took out a cigarette. She reached for the other ashtray, a cast-iron model as big as a soup bowl. On this one two GIs raised a gray flag.

"Were you in the war?" Marian asked.

Jerome shook his head. "I contributed tires and batteries," he said.

In the kitchen Gootie imitated Marian inhaling a Pall Mall, staining the cigarette paper with her painted red lips.

"I knew two fatalities," Marian said.

Jerome nodded his head in sympathy.

"They were heroes," Marian said.

"This is an engagement," Gootie whispered to me, "not a funeral." She sent me to the dining room with another plate full of sponge cake cut into thick slices.

"What does your grandma think we are?" Marian Goldman giggled. She put one of the slices on her plate. "He's a little doll, isn't he?" She kissed the top of my head.

"I see you're a good boy," Jerome said. "You help your grandma."

I looked at him closely, wondering if I too would end up courting a Marian Goldman.

Gootie said they would become engaged right away. "Neither has anything to lose," she said. "If they wait too long, they'll get a match with the angel of death."

"The cake is pareve," I said.

Jerome looked at me.

"It means neutral," Marian said, "neither meat nor milk. This family observes the old ways. I'm much more modern."

"Modern," Gootie whispered to me. "She thinks he'll marry her because she's modern. The cat and dog are modern, too—they don't need a wedding. They just go out into the street."

Gootie liked Jerome. He reminded her of her brothers—all three were rural fellows; even Leo, the millionaire, lived in the tiny town of Alma.

Jerome took out his handkerchief. I peeked through the kitchen door.

"This is it," Gootie said. "He's going to ask her to grab one end. He'll hold the other and it will be official. They'll become engaged. That's just how I did it."

Smoke flowed from Marian Goldman's nostrils and from her red lips.

"If he's smart," Gootie said, "he'll ask her first if she can still have children. If not is not. He'll still have a wife—that's better than living like a stone."

Rocky hated matchmaking and any other intrigues. He liked to work and pray and read from the oversize books that he kept upstairs in a bookcase with glass doors. Gootie never let him in on any of her plans.

Rocky knew about Jerome from Evart, but not the matchmaking. He woke up, walked into the dining room. He smelled the smoke; then he saw the giggling, heavyset daughter of Goldman, whom he didn't like.

"What's going on here?" he said. "You're stinking up the house with cigarettes. If you want to smoke, go outside or to your own house."

Marian Goldman crushed her cigarette. She picked up her purse. "I'm sorry," she said. "It's a pleasure to meet you," she told Jerome. They shook hands.

Gootie had tears in her eyes. By the time she got to the scene, Marian was gone and Jerome had put the handkerchief back in his pocket. Then he put on his hat and left.

"This was a match," Gootie said. "This was destiny until you came in. Even if you pray and do good deeds for ten years, you won't make up for the damage you just did to two souls. You stopped a wedding. Because of a cigarette you stopped a wedding."

"If they want a wedding," Rocky said, "they can go to the Polish Falcons Hall and have a wedding. Smoking, drinking, anything they want. Not here."

"In the heavens," Gootie said, "they're crying over the children these two might have had."

"It's true," I said. "He had his handkerchief ready. I saw it."

"Look what you're teaching him," Rocky said. "He'd be better off listening to the radio. Go away from her," he said. "Go listen to the radio before she drives you crazy."

Chapter 7

*O*n the radio I heard stories. The Lone Ranger and Tonto tracked criminals across the badlands on horseback. Sky King chased them by helicopter, the Green Hornet by car. When I translated for her, Gootie liked to listen with me. She howled over the Lone Ranger, a man who walked around wearing a mask. "You think people didn't know who he was?" she said. To prove it she stripped a piece of cloth from her handkerchief. We cut holes for eyes. I put the mask on, then she did. We recognized each other without a problem. About the Indian, she was less certain. "What is an Indian?" she wanted to know. I wasn't sure myself; I only knew they were the opposite of cowboys.

Gootie decided that Tonto was an Andalusian. She had known lots of them in Odessa. They had round faces and slanted eyes, and a lot of them drove horse wagons. He must have been a good-hearted man, she decided. "Who else would go all over with the crazy one who wears a mask? They don't tell you on the radio, but people must have followed him around like they follow all clowns."

In Serei there had been a village idiot, Todres. "You think he didn't wear a mask? Plenty of times," Gootie said, "and if he'd had a white horse, he would have galloped around Serei on the horse instead of pulling a goat on a rope. But even Todres, weak in the brain as he was, would never carry a gun."

She couldn't understand why the Green Hornet needed a mask, or Batman, or, in the funny page that I read to her every Sunday, why the Phantom covered his face.

"What are they ashamed of?" Gootie wanted to know. "The criminals wear hats with feathers and fancy suits, and the ones who help the police wear pajamas and cover their faces."

We didn't divide the world into true or false or fact or fiction. Everything was a story, and some stories required other stories to explain them. History and reality were not our concern. We just wanted to know what happened next.

"Before Moses died," Gootie said, "God told him to climb on a hill. He looked at the land of Israel that he would never live to enter, and then before he died God showed him everything. 'Moses,' God said, 'it's a shame that you can't go into Israel, and it's a shame that you can't live forever or even hundreds of years like people used to. But before you die have a look—here's every-thing that's going to happen between now and the time Moshi-ach [the Messiah] comes when the dead will return and everyone will make a good living.'

"Moses, standing on the mountain, saw everything. Do you think he was surprised by radios and televisions and cars and air-planes? Don't be silly. These things are nothing. If he had said, 'God, please give your people radios or televisions,' do you think God would have denied Moses—the only person he ever spoke to face-to-face? Never. But Moses was a smart man. He didn't ask for silliness. He asked for good health for his people, and even this has not been easy, not even for God."

The stories about God were not so different from the stories about people. In a certain way God was in all the stories; he allowed them to happen. The way he showed Moses everything, he showed the rest of us a sliver, a fingernail of reality.

" 'God,' Moses said before he died, 'can I live not as a person but as a fly, just long enough to enter the land of Israel?' "

Gootie usually shed a tear for Moses at this point in the story. "Even as a fly," she said, "imagine the greatest man in the world ready to live as a fly, and he couldn't."

We could start with the Lone Ranger and go to Moses, to Serei, to the poker players my father caroused with—stories blended; one thing led to another. You had to be careful in America about what to believe.

When we got our own television everyone in the neighborhood came to see it. Ours was the first one on the block. Izzy Danto, my father's friend from Detroit, once a gambler himself, had settled down and owned a furniture store. He brought us the TV in the back of his station wagon. We plugged it in and saw men in short pants throwing each other around. "I wouldn't give you a nickel for it," Gootie said.

Izzy defended it. "People are lining up outside the store," he said. "I can sell as many TVs as they ship to me."

Like my father, Izzy had lost his hair as a young man, but this loss had not weakened him. He lifted the heavy console by himself to give us a better picture away from the glare of the sun. He tinkered with the antenna.

For the first weeks our neighbors came for the evening. People filled all the chairs; the children sat on the floor. During *Arthur Godfrey and His Friends* they gossiped in Polish, but for wrestling everyone paid attention and cheered. Gootie stayed in the kitchen. Only much later did she consider watching television. After the crowd dissipated, after the neighbors had their own sets and boxing and wrestling no longer dominated the evenings, Gootie began to watch *I Love Lucy*. She paid attention. "This," she said, "this is something to see." She dabbed at her eyes.

"It's a funny program," I told her.

"What do you know," she said. "If they told you dog poop was a potato pancake, you'd believe it, as long as it was something they told you in school."

Every Monday night I insisted that Lucy was a gentile.

"She has a Jewish face," Gootie said, "and Jewish ways."

I read aloud to her articles from the newspaper about Lucille Ball whenever I found them. Nobody called her Jewish.

"Of course they don't tell you," Gootie said. "Do you think they'd keep her on television if she told everyone?"

Gootie knew how to read the signs. First, Lucy wasn't her real name. Her real name was Rootie. Another sign Gootie detected in the bedroom. "They don't sleep in the same bed," she pointed out, because in spite of everything she did to disguise her origins, Rootie had not forgotten the laws of family purity.

As for Ricky Ricardo, Gootie had nothing against him: he dressed well; he was polite. She almost understood how the gullible Rootie had fallen in love with him. "What did she know?" Gootie conjectured. "She was probably not the kind of girl who listened to a mother. She went away to school; she saw him every day; he gave her presents; she wasn't smart enough to see what he wanted. One day he took her out to the fields. When she cried out for help he said, 'Rootie, I love you.' In America everybody says 'I love you,' then they think it's all right to do anything they want. After that Rootie couldn't look her mother in the face. She didn't think any other man would marry her. The girl was so young and already she thought her life was over.

"Had she told her mother, they could have done something. There are plenty of Jewish men who would have married her anyway—free thinkers, Communists, orphans, men who are themselves no bargains—but Rootie ran away with him to a priest. They woke the priest in the middle of the night; he unlocked the church and sprinkled her with holy water. She couldn't stay in the same city, so she moved away, and now after being married all these years she has no children, a curse from God, and she still lives in an apartment because Ricky Ricardo, for all his kisses and I love yous, has never come up with the down payment for a house."

This, Gootie convinced herself, was the true story of Rootie. Every week, for people like me, they made up silliness about Fred and Ethel, and they stopped in the middle to tell you to go to the store to buy soap or Coca-Cola, and people all over America sat in front of television sets and laughed. What was there to laugh at? Rootie's parents were not laughing. They lived the rest of their lives in anguish, and for her dead ancestors it was worse. Life didn't stop with the living.

Our relatives, Gootie said, were all over the place in heaven, trying to intercede with fate on our behalf. They advised God to take it easy on punishment; they recited our good deeds. The great ones, Moses and Abraham and the Prophet Elijah, were like the kings and presidents on earth, busy plotting the big moves for eternity. But our family, Gootie's mother and father in particular, never tired of reminding God about us and about all the people of Serei. Yes, they were dead, but they were still parents.

We had nothing to fear from our dead, and they had only one thing to fear from us. We could have them banished behind the black curtain. Rootie had done this to her ancestors, and even if everyone in the country loved her and watched her on Monday night, she could never atone for what she had done to the grand-parents and great-grandparents, the hardworking dead who had been sitting at God's right hand, demanding a break for Rootie, for the Jewish people, for all innocents and sufferers.

Your ancestors could trust you not to kill or steal or worship idols; if you did those sorts of things, even the dead couldn't help you out. The danger to them lay in only one deed: marriage. If you married a gentile, it affected the dead. Suddenly they became the grandparents of gentiles. They had to remove themselves from the part of heaven that was like Serei and go behind the black curtain.

In that territory the dead knew shame. And what good did it do you? Did Rootie find happiness? Never, no matter what she did, no matter how many times Ricky Ricardo said "I love you" or "babaloo" and kissed her cheek, she thought about her ancestors pining away behind the black curtain.

I thought about the black curtain a lot, and once I thought I saw it in the Union High auditorium. My sister Bailey performed in a Latin Club play. Gootie and I were in the audience. The curtain moved, and I saw Bailey and her friends in white sheets, speaking words I couldn't understand. In the junior high Latin Club I recognized my ancestors, ghosts in sheets, wondering whom I'd marry.

"The black curtain," I whispered to Gootie, "just like in the other world."

"Not the same," Gootie said, "but you're beginning to understand."

Chapter 8

When the baker's union finally forced Rocky to retire, we all worried. He had too much energy to sit still. "Give me a piece of work," he asked my father, "anything."

My father had a short-wheelbase Dodge truck. He drove to machine shops and small factories in western Michigan to buy scrap metal and steel.

"If he could drive," my father said, "I'd let him. But he wants to load the truck—I can't let an old man load steel."

"Why not?" Rocky said. He went to Woolworth's and bought himself a pair of cotton jersey gloves. One day when my father opened the cab of his Dodge he found Rocky inside waiting for him.

"Let's go," Rocky said.

My father told us what happened.

"I didn't want to hurt his feelings. I know how much he wants to work, so I let him go along for the ride. I was going to go out of town, but instead I went to Michigan Fleet. They've always got something outside. When I went to the office I told him to stay in the truck. When I came out, it couldn't have been ten minutes later, he'd probably thrown five hundred pounds of steel clippings onto the truck. I made him stop.

"'They've got a crane; you don't have to do this.'

"'Who needs a crane?' he said. 'This is light stuff.' He was throwing on chunks that only weighed four or five pounds each, but they were sharp corrugated pieces that they use to make gas tanks. The men on break teased me. 'You getting the old man to do your work, Sammy?' . . . Before I could get the crane operator to come over, he had done half the job by hand. I can't take him along. He could really hurt himself in some of the factories."

Gootie said my father didn't want Rocky because he was ashamed. "Sam thinks he's a big shot now because he's got his name on the truck."

I defended my father. "He had to do it; he got a ticket. If you have a business truck, it's got to have a name on it."

"Go on," Gootie said. "He put his name on to show off. But I don't blame Sam for not taking him anymore—the little devil could cause trouble anyplace."

When my father wouldn't let him into the cab, Rocky sulked. He took it out on the kids in the neighborhood. He patrolled as if he were a cop walking the beat. If anyone broke a Coke bottle, he made them clean it up. He chased away dogs he didn't recognize. Teenage boys had to hide their cigarettes when they saw him coming. Larry Hayes, who lived across the street in the house Rocky and Gootie had abandoned after Max's death, had a particularly bad time.

Larry didn't work, either. He was not even forty, but he had a military pension. His wife worked as a maid. Rocky hated to see a strong man sit in front of his house and tinker with a motorcycle. He had hated Larry for years. Suddenly they had become equals. For much of the day they saw one another. Larry, with a beer in one hand and a gun magazine across his belly, sat in a ripped chaise longue and kept an eye on his kids, who were usually nowhere in sight. Rocky, sitting on his own porch or patrolling the block, couldn't avoid him. Larry made the mistake of pointing out their similarity.

"Rocky," he said, "you and me both got all day to kill. Have a beer."

"You should choke on your beer," Rocky said. "Pick up the bottles."

Larry wore his T-shirt rolled to the shoulder and kept his cigarettes in the sleeve. A tattoo on one arm said "Iwo Jima." On the other he had a Hawaiian dancing girl. His belly weighed more than Rocky.

"Get a job," Rocky told him a hundred times, and Larry always had the same answer.

"Landlord," he said, "I'm a sick man."

"You're a lazy man."

Larry laughed. "I'm lazy, too—you're right about that."

"And good for nothing," Rocky added.

"Good for drinking," Larry said, "and you know what else." He pointed to the Hawaiian girl on his forearm.

Evicting Larry became Rocky's goal. Gootie refused. "He has a wife and children," she said, "and he pays the rent. Why is it your business what he does all day? Forget about him."

Rocky couldn't. Right before his eyes sat the living symbol of what he hated—laziness. Larry tried to keep his motorcycle parts and beer bottles more orderly, but he couldn't satisfy Rocky.

"Either you call a sheriff to evict him," Rocky announced to Gootie, "or I go in there and throw his things into the street."

"You can't evict a man who fought Hitler," Gootie said.

"He fought Hitler like you fought Hitler. I want him out of the house."

"Not as long as I live," Gootie said. "Are you going to evict a man with four little children?"

"One of them is already in a juvenile home," Rocky said. "And the others will be, too," he predicted, "and then straight to jail. Tomorrow I'm going to the city attorney and I'm getting him an eviction notice."

"It's because he's not working," Gootie told me. She said we had to find him something to do. "Thank God there's *Shabbes* and he has to rest at least one day. For him God should have made seven Sabbaths."

The next day, before he left for City Hall to get an eviction notice, Gootie asked Rocky to bake. She had put out the flour, the rolling pin, the yeast, the eggs. Rocky was wearing his brown suit to impress the municipal officials. He was suspicious. At home, Gootie never let him bake.

Seeing all the ingredients laid out made it tempting.

"All of a sudden you want me to bake," he said. "All of a sudden the store bread isn't good enough for you."

"Not all of a sudden," Gootie said. "When you were working I wanted you to rest when you were home. Now you've got time."

"I always had time," Rocky said. "You're like your mother; you never knew what a good piece of bread was, and you'll never know."

"Then bake a few loaves for everyone else in the family."

"Leave everything out," he said. "I'll bake after I serve him the eviction papers. When I get rid of that lazy son of a bitch I'll bake a cake like you never tasted."

"Bake something now," she said, "for the child." She pointed to me. I knew what she was doing. So did Rocky.

"Later," he said.

"Not later," Gootie said. She blocked the door with her body and used a powerful phrase: "*Es shmekt im.*" It meant a hunger, a taste for a certain food that if unsatisfied could lead to a quick and certain death. If a person had this hankering, this *shmek*, you had to supply the food he wanted at once. In Serei at a wedding an uninvited onlooker once died from inhaling the aroma of roasted chicken. For that reason, at Gootie's wedding and all others, everyone in town shared in the wedding feast. There was an example in the Torah as well. Esau gave up his birthright in exchange for Jacob's lentil soup. It says right in the Torah that if Esau didn't taste the soup, he would have died.

We respected the doctrine. If anyone walked into our house to use the telephone and there was aromatic food cooking, they had to eat even if they didn't want to. We couldn't risk killing them.

"You want a piece of my bread that bad?" Rocky asked me.

Gootie answered for me. "Look at him. The wind could carry him away. He can't eat what Philip and Joe Post bake, and the challah from Detroit gives him diarrhea. They freeze it, and who knows what's in the freezer with it?"

Rocky took off his jacket and put on an apron. He knew he was being had, but the chance to bake overwhelmed him. He was the one who had the powerful longing. After he baked four challahs, Gootie told him we needed more. He would have to make a new dough. She sent him to the A&P for more flour. After the bread had cooled Gootie cut a slice of egg challah. She and I both tasted.

"It's the Garden of Eden," she said.

"It's just a piece of bread," he said, "but a good piece."

"Nobody but you can bake like this," she said. "Why don't you take a few loaves to Joe Peters's store? The Polacks will buy it, and you can bake at home every day."

Rocky and I went to the IGA store. Joe Peters was dead, but everyone still called it his store. The latest in a string of new owners, Mr. Boersma, a Dutchman in a butcher's apron, had taken over the store a few months earlier. He was out of place in a Polish neighborhood. He kept the shelves clean and charged too much. We always shopped at the A&P. Rocky grabbed a loaf of sliced white bread. He put it on the counter and squeezed the air out of it. The grocer punched in the price on his register.

"You call this bread?" Rocky asked.

"Most people do," Boersma said.

Rocky held up his challah. "*This* is a bread."

Boersma agreed.

"How many you want?" Rocky asked. "Two, three dozen? I'll bake as many as you can sell."

Boersma said he didn't think he could sell any.

"People will line up to buy it," Rocky said. "You know how

many eggs are in the dough? Four—and whole, not powdered. You can't buy a bread like this."

Boersma rarely spoke unless you asked him the price of something. He had only two aisles, and when kids entered the store he walked out from behind the register so he could watch every move. He didn't know how to respond to Rocky. He looked to me for help.

"It's good bread," I told him.

"I order everything from IGA," he said. "I can't buy from people who walk in. There's all kinds of rules—Health Department, you know—"

Rocky interrupted him. "I worked in the American Bakery forty years. You think I don't know how to wash my hands?"

I tried to pull him toward the door. The grocer stood beside his cash register, his arms folded. The packaged white bread lay in front of him.

"You gonna buy this bread?" he asked.

"I wouldn't take it for nothing," Rocky said.

"Then why'd you squeeze it?" the grocer said. "Now nobody will buy it."

"Good," Rocky said, "I'll go squeeze them all."

Boersma walked from behind the counter to protect his white bread. Rocky broke loose from my grip and reached the bread display. Before Mr. Boersma could stop him, Rocky had his hands on another loaf of Holsum bread. He held it up and squeezed it as if there were an audience, but only the grocer and I watched.

"You should be ashamed to sell this," Rocky said. "Send it back. They won't make you pay for it."

The grocer pulled the white bread from Rocky's grip.

"Get out," he said, "and don't come here unless you're gonna buy something."

I handed Rocky the challah. For a minute I thought he was going to hit Boersma with it, but he just walked out.

"Don't ever go there again," he told me.

We went to the Red and White store on Front Street and

then to an independent grocery store. Rocky didn't squeeze any more breads, but he didn't sell his, either.

That evening I told Gootie what had happened. She asked me to call Philip, his cousin, who still owned the American Bakery.

"He's going to drive our tenant, who fought Hitler, into the streets," she told Philip, "and the sin will be on your head. God knows what he'll do after that."

Philip said he couldn't put Rocky back to work. The union would close his shop if he broke the rules.

"Everybody eats bread," Gootie said. "There's a city full of bakeries—can't you find somebody who will take him? Even if they don't pay him. I don't care if he bakes for the Salvation Army."

Philip came over to visit. He took Rocky for a ride in his Buick. They didn't return until after dark. The next day Rocky didn't wait for me outside Turner School as he had started to do, and he wasn't home at noon, either, to eat his big meal. Gootie looked out the window, expecting Larry and his family to be squatting on the sidewalk; but the tenant drank his beer in peace.

When Rocky came home in the middle of the afternoon he went right to sleep, his old schedule.

We telephoned Philip again. "You're a holy man," Gootie said, "even though you live like an atheist. Even the greatest rabbi couldn't do what you did."

"I just drove him," Philip said. "He did the rest himself."

Twice a week, in the middle of the night, Rocky walked two miles to the Holsum Bread Company. At the nonunion bakery, he oversaw the ovens that baked the air-filled white bread that was packaged in white plastic and shipped all over the city. His bread did end up in the IGA store after all, but none of us teased him about it.

Chapter 9

*A*t school I learned things about health that Gootie said were wrong. The teacher passed out free half-pints of milk at snack time. Everyone else drank. My mother told me to drink. The teacher told me to drink.

"Go ahead," Gootie said. "Milk is fine if you want to wake up the worms that are lying in your intestines just waiting to torture you."

I drank, and I worried that Gootie would die because she never drank milk and didn't have the strong bones and muscles the school nurse told us about. But I worried most about what Gootie called her *keelie*, her hernia. I watched for trouble, and I knew how to read the signs. When it was time, I went with her to Mr. Cooper's office.

My job, as always, was to translate, but there wasn't much need. Mr. Cooper knew what to do. Gootie sat on the folding chair in his outer office and raised her dress, exposing her pale orange slip, which was like another dress. Mr. Cooper reached around her back and carefully pulled at the steel band that encircled her lower abdomen.

"Meester Cooper," Gootie said in her best attempt at 100 percent English, "thank you. You are every time safing mine leben."

In his dingy office surrounded by three armless and legless department store dummies, Cooper looked surprisingly healthy. He was in his forties, with hair combed back and slicked down with the Wildroot Cream Oil he kept in the bathroom. He always wore a bow tie.

I stood ready to translate, but Cooper clicked his tongue and said only formulaic things like "We'll see about that" or "I'll just be a minute or two" or "This doesn't look so bad," phrases Gootie could understand just by his tone of voice. Still, I was glad to be there and lobbied for the job, convinced my mother that it was more important than third or fourth grade for the hour or two every few months that these adjustments required. I could tell by my own observations when the time to see Mr. Cooper approached. When, as we talked at night, Gootie would have to stand to pull at the belt from time to time, or when she adjusted the leather pads at both sides of her abdomen, then I knew what we had to do; but I always waited until Gootie said it was time. If I suggested Mr. Cooper, she always found a reason to delay.

In spite of the way she praised him in her opening English sentence, Gootie didn't like Mr. Cooper. "He charges five dollars for every little thing," she said, "but what can I do? He keeps me together."

Like so much else in our family history, Gootie's hernia originated in Max's death—on the very day she and Bashy walked into the funeral parlor. Bashy took one look at her dead brother and collapsed. Gootie bent to pick up her daughter. At that moment her innards gave way, putting her forever after at the mercy of Mr. Cooper and his trusses.

"Hernia" was the fancy word that we used in Cooper's office or on the telephone. At home we called it a "rupture." To me the steel-and-padded-leather band around Gootie's abdomen was a mark of her heroism—the way she had persevered after her son's death. It was like the colorful decorations the veterans wore on their uniforms. We had three veterans on our block. Eugene and Tommy Long lived with their widowed mother. Every Sunday they put on their uniforms decorated with ribbons and colorful bands and walked their proud mother to St. Ann's Church for mass. When they passed our house I liked to stand on the porch and salute. They saluted back and waved as if they were in a parade.

The other veteran was Larry, Rocky's enemy.

"His wife told me," Gootie said, "that down there he's held together by wires. Three times the poor man has had ruptures. You can't expect a man like that to keep a job; any minute the wires could break."

Cooper came out of his workshop one day holding Gootie's truss in his arms like a puppy. He spoke to me so that I could translate.

"I'm so sorry," he said. "I couldn't fix it this time. It's just gone. It's very old. They can't last forever."

Before I translated, I panicked.

"What will hold my grandma together?"

"She'll have to get a new one," Mr. Cooper said. "It won't take that long to make it up; I've got her measurements."

When I translated for Gootie, she motioned with her hands and told Cooper in Yiddish to fix this one.

"Tell your grandma I can't do it," Mr. Cooper said to me. "Tell her it's worn out. No good. Finished."

"Feex," Gootie said.

Mr. Cooper shook his head.

I knew what Gootie's question would be, so I asked. The truss maker shrugged his shoulders.

"It's expensive all right," he said, "maybe seventy-five dollars, maybe more. But you can pay it out five dollars a week if you want."

"Feex," Gootie said again. She took the truss out of his arms and wrapped it around herself. She stood and sucked in her breath.

"She says it's fine," I told Mr. Cooper.

"Fine right now," Mr. Cooper said. "It may stay fine for an hour, a day, a week. Who knows?"

"And then what happens?"

Cooper looked at Gootie standing between two torsos modeling his work. He made a cracking sound and showed me a break with his hands. He meant the truss, but I took it to mean Gootie.

On the bus ride home I could tell that she was worried. She didn't talk.

"Seventy-five dollars isn't so much," I said.

"Go on, he lies. It will be more, and then who knows how long it will last. He doesn't guarantee it for an hour."

"You've got to have a new one," I insisted. "I'm going to tell Bashy."

"Don't start up," Gootie warned me, "or it will be the end of me. They'll put me in the hospital, cut me open, and you'll never see me again."

My mother and Dr. Schnorr always told her to have an operation. Gootie preferred the truss to the surgeon's knife, and I didn't blame her. Still, if I kept our secret, one day Cooper's prediction would come true—there would be the cracking sound followed by Gootie coming apart. I decided that I wasn't going to leave her. If the truss broke, I would keep her together until Bashy and Dr. Schnorr and an ambulance could get her to a hospital.

I tried not to hover; I just stayed around the house and kept my eye on her. Nobody noticed anything unusual, but I lived under great pressure. After a few days I needed help. I went across the street to consult the expert. I waited until he looked up so I wouldn't disturb him. Since I couldn't get right to the point, I warmed up with small talk.

"Did you really fight Hitler?" I asked.

"Yup," Larry said. "I sure did. Wiped out a lot of those bastards," he said nonchalantly. I went on to the next subject.

"Are you held together by wire down there?"

This seemed to engage him more than Hitler had. He put down his magazine and thought about it.

"I guess I am," he said. "Who told you?"

I didn't answer because I didn't want to implicate Gootie. Larry didn't press me.

"Did you come for a motorcycle ride?" he asked.

"No," I said. "I'm not allowed."

"Too bad," he said. "You Jews are missing out on a good thing."

I agreed.

"Rocky send you over?"

"No," I said, "nobody sent me. I came to talk about the wires."

"Not that much to say," he said. "Everybody's got trouble. John D. Rockefeller, the millionaire, hasn't even got a stomach."

I wanted to be ready in case Gootie needed me. "Where do you get the wire?"

"You can't just buy it," he said. "The doctors give it to you. And it's not really wire—they just call it that. It's made from a cat's guts, you know, like a violin string."

"My grandma's got a rupture," I said.

"It's no wonder," he said. "Living with Rocky would give anybody a rupture." He laughed and picked up his magazine.

"I'm afraid she'll come apart."

"Nah," he said. "A rupture's not as bad as you think. I've had three."

"I know," I said, "you're a bigger hero than Eugene and Tommy Long."

This pleased Larry. "They're not heroes," he said. "They're assholes. You're okay, Junior. Don't let Rocky get to you."

"If it happens," I asked, "if she starts to come apart, how will I hold her together?"

I had nothing specific in mind. I didn't expect Gootie to explode like a firecracker, but coming apart meant something real to me. I understood dissolution without having an image of it. What had begun beside Max's coffin might return at any moment. Mr. Cooper had warned us. I had to be ready.

"You mean if the hernia pops?" he asked. "If that happens, you just push it back in place." He demonstrated by pressing on a huge glob of his belly. I watched a wave of fat ripple.

"How will I know where to push?"

"That's not a job for a kid," Larry said. "Tell your grandma to ask me herself. I'll explain it to her."

That evening I told Gootie about my conversation with Larry.

"You shouldn't have said anything. He'll tell everyone I've got a rupture."

"But I can't keep staying home from school," I said, "and somebody has to help you when the belt goes." I tried to imitate the cracking sound Mr. Cooper had made.

"I didn't know you were so worried about the rupture," Gootie said.

The next day we went to the bank. Gootie hated to do it, but once a month we had to. She held the little blue bankbook, and I made out the withdrawal form. On our monthly trips it was always ten dollars. The tellers knew us. Everyone was friendly, but Gootie couldn't hide her nervousness. She played with the rubber band that she kept around the bankbook; her eyes scanned what was happening behind the teller's barred window.

She trusted no institutions, not governments, not synagogues, and above all not banks. She had seen her Lithuanian money turn worthless after World War I, and in 1929 she'd lost $185 when a bank collapsed.

She kept her money in a handkerchief, knotted many times and then placed in the locked cedar chest in her closet where she stored her wedding apron, the leg brace she had worn in Odessa, and pictures of Eser and his children. When she reached $100 she let Bashy deposit the money in the bank in order to save us from thieves. She didn't think thieves would bother with less than $100, but for a hundred they might come in and kill us all.

Every month we kept the bank honest. Gootie withdrew ten dollars to make sure they'd really give it to us. She didn't relax until the teller handed us a ten-dollar bill. She looked at it, and without giving up our place in line, she told me to redeposit the money.

"We're doing everyone a favor," Gootie said. "The bank knows we're watching them."

One of the tellers had our usual ten waiting for us. We surprised her when we withdrew seventy-five for Mr. Cooper. Gootie wrapped it in a handkerchief.

In his office, Mr. Cooper looked away while she counted. I handed over the cash.

"She wants a good one," I said, "even if it costs more."

"You bet," Mr. Cooper said.

Gootie grabbed my arm, whispered to me. "Up to five dollars more," I said, "that's all."

"I'll make her the best," the truss man said. "Don't worry."

"Don't talk to Larry anymore about my *keelie*," Gootie said, "or to anybody else."

I didn't, and when Mr. Cooper fitted her into the seventy-five-dollar truss I stopped worrying about her health.

Chapter 10

When my mother read Gootie the letter that I handed to her she yelled, "*Gevalt.*"

"Quick, get me the smelling salts," Gootie said.

I ran to her bedroom for the tiny bottle of colored crystals that she held under her nose on Yom Kippur to keep her from fainting. I knew it was an important letter because it came in a blue foreign envelope.

"Who's it from?"

"From the dead," Gootie answered. She inhaled deeply from the little bottle. My mother and I helped her to her bed.

"Is it from Eserkey?" I asked my mother.

"I wish," Bashy said, "but he's dead for sure. This is from Miriam, a cousin. I don't remember her."

The next day Joe drove in from Muskegon to see the letter.

"After you don't hear from someone for half a lifetime, is this the kind of letter you write?" Gootie asked. "I saw Miriam every day. She would know how to write a letter to me. After I left for

America she used to write. She told me what was happening in Serei, how everyone was—not four lines in English."

Gootie decided it was a different Miriam who had somehow found Gootie's name and was busy looking for people in America who might send her money.

Rocky believed that it was Miriam. He said we should send money even if she hadn't asked for any. Gootie's brother Leo discussed the matter with his children, and they too decided it was the real Miriam; but Joe and Gootie continued to think it was an impostor. The letter didn't mention any other names.

"The real Miriam would have said, 'Say hello to Joe, to Louie,'" Joe said. "She would have wanted to know about everyone, and she would have written in Yiddish the way she always did."

For weeks Miriam's letter dominated the household. Finally Leo decided to call. After many attempts a foreign operator told him there was no phone for a Miriam Wasserman in Haifa.

Long before the letter came we had been talking about Palestine. My father went to meetings that were not at the synagogue. He came home much earlier than from poker games. He looked solemn and talked about President Truman.

Rocky said that, President Truman or no President Truman, Israel would return when God wanted it to happen, not when the UN decided. There was a lot of talk about the war. I had trouble following. The American war was no problem. It was over. At Marvel Surplus you could buy uniforms, navy or army caps, bullet casings, bayonets, and even German Lugers, the long-barreled pistols that our soldiers had brought back as trophies. At Turner School the boys talked about these things; some of them even wore navy or army caps.

At home we talked about the First World War and the Arab-Israel war as if they happened at the same time. I didn't know battle details, only what happened to people in our family—people like Eserkey and Miriam.

My father wrote Gootie's return letter in English and in Yiddish. He wrote how happy we were to know that Miriam was alive. He sent a picture of our family posed at the wedding of Leo's daughter in Bay City. He asked for more information.

While we waited, my father came home from a meeting with news about Palestine. He gave me a little blue-and-white flag. "This is Israel's," he said.

Gootie didn't understand what was going on. "There always has been Israel," she said. "There always has been Jerusalem. The souls of the dead from all over the world go directly to Yerushalayim [Jerusalem]. That's the first stop. From there God sorts them out, and then they go all over. The lucky ones stay in Yerushalayim."

My father said there was a war in Israel with real soldiers and guns. Gootie doubted it. Then the second letter from Miriam came. It included a picture of her son-in-law in the uniform of an Israeli soldier. He was a heavyset man, not as young as the men in uniform I saw on the streets of Grand Rapids. There was also a picture that made Gootie cry. Miriam stared at us in black and white. Not only alive, but an old lady with bags under her eyes, the right Miriam. "To my dear Gootie," she wrote in Yiddish on the back of the photo. "Thank God that you're alive, too."

That evening Gootie sat down to write. I had never seen her do so before. She cleared the table of food, washed and dried the surface, then she asked me to find her a pencil and paper. Her lips moved. She asked me to leave; she didn't like me to watch.

After my father addressed the envelope, I carried it to the mailbox. Every day Gootie waited for an answer. When Miriam's letter finally arrived, we gathered around the dining room table. My father held the letter in one hand and read each Yiddish sentence slowly.

"I walked," Miriam wrote. "My little girl and I walked. The Nazis were always after us. We followed the Russian soldiers. We ate what we could, sometimes nothing. Along the way my husband died. After the war they sent us to Cyprus and now I'm in Haifa. I didn't write to you," she said, "because I was afraid. Ever since they killed everybody I've been afraid I don't know of what, of everything. I was afraid you would be dead too. I didn't want to know."

Every month or two Gootie sent a package. She made us go through our clothes and give some to Miriam and her family. She pestered her brothers to send money. She didn't have to try very hard. Even Joe, who bought nothing for himself, went to the post office and sent international money orders to Miriam in Haifa.

Gootie and I had trouble figuring out exactly where Miriam was. On the big globe that I brought to the kitchen table, I found Palestine, a yellow dot the size of a fingernail. Gootie couldn't even see it, and there was no Haifa.

"Look for Serei," Gootie said.

I spun the world left and right. I read as many place names as I could decipher aloud to her. I did find Odessa.

"They put Odessa on to fool you," Gootie said, "so you'll think all the cities are like that. Thank God they're not. Who needs Odessa, filled with Communists and gangsters and street-walkers. They should have forgotten Odessa and put Serei there."

I couldn't even find Lithuania, so we put aside the globe and Gootie tried to understand what happened and where Miriam was without any mechanical devices.

"When I left for America," Gootie said, "Miriam wasn't married yet. She came to help me pack the trunks. Miriam said maybe she would come to America too someday, but first she wanted to get married in Serei. Nobody wanted to marry an American man; nobody wanted to marry an Odessa man, either. In the big cities you couldn't know who anybody really was.

"Miriam opened the trunk and the first thing she put in was my wedding dress. 'I'll come back for your wedding,' I told her . . . people think and God laughs . . . her wedding. I don't even know what her husband's name was. And now he's dead and she's an old woman living somewhere near Yerushalayim. You see what can happen."

My father said it was more important to send money to help Israel than it was to help Miriam. "If there's no Israel, if they lose the war, she won't have a place to live," my father said.

"If she has a dollar," Gootie said, "she'll have a place."

Gootie prayed for Miriam. She spoke directly to God: not in Hebrew, not in the prayers that were in holy books; she addressed him directly in Yiddish. "*Ribeynu shel olam* [Lord of the World]," she said, "Miriam has had enough trouble for one life, and there have been enough wars and enough Hitlers. Let her live out her years there close to Yerushalayim. Amen."

Gootie opened her eyes. We drank coffee after she prayed. I was sure God listened.

"She'll be all right," Gootie said, "and when she dies her soul won't even have to travel very far."

After Gootie's prayer there was still war in Israel and letters full of Miriam's sorrow. We sent clothing and money, but no matter what happened I never worried about Miriam. In the place we couldn't find on the globe she was absolutely safe. Gootie guaranteed it.

Chapter 11

*I*n our family of immigrants my father seemed most American. He spoke without an accent, and he could read and write in fluent English. When I watched him shoot pool, or when I sat beside him at a Grand Rapids Jets baseball game, I thought we were as American as any father and son could be.

He took me to sporting events throughout the year. In the winter we had the Rockets, a minor league hockey team. In the summer we had three baseball teams to follow: the Jets, the Chicks in the girls' league, and the Detroit Wolves in the Negro league, who played a lot of their home games in Grand Rapids. Sam loved sports as much as Rocky loved Talmud study. I could hardly believe that he had been born in Poland and didn't come to America until he was nineteen.

He ended up in Michigan after he lost all his money betting on the 1927 Pirates. He met Bashy while she was in Detroit visiting cousins. Sam showed up for a poker game.

"She should have known then," Gootie said. "Who meets a

groom at a gambling place? She was eighteen," Gootie told me, "and he was already losing his hair. But what could I do? She didn't listen to me like I didn't listen to my mother. He would be all right," she said, "if he wasn't a gambler."

Two or three times a week, after he ate and showered, my father, looking like a lawyer or businessman in his sport shirt and slacks, went out to play poker. Gootie, who approved of him in work clothes, turned away from "*der* gambler," the name she called him when he wasn't home.

He laughed off her nickname, but I couldn't. I knew from her Serei stories what a gambler did. He snuck away from work to play cards or shoot dice. He stayed out until all hours of the night. He drank. His friends were all gamblers, too. His wife begged him to stop, but he didn't. He gambled away the grocery money. He bought whiskey instead of milk for the children. His wife left him. His family ended up in the poorhouse. He died a beggar.

When Gootie called my father "*der* gambler," I saw the whole picture, and some of it had already come to pass. At the barbershop, where my father placed bets, all his friends did the same. He did stay out late at night, and sometimes when he took me to one of the factories where he picked up scrap, I watched him play cards with the workers. It was just the way Gootie said. The whistle would blow for a ten-minute coffee break, and the men couldn't wait to gamble. They turned over boxes to make seats right beside their machines. They pulled out a deck and began to deal as fast as they could to get in the full measure of gambling in those ten minutes. My father pulled off his gloves and joined. He supplied the decks. The factory workers with their grimy fingers didn't care if the cards had been handled by lawyers or salesmen a few days before. They thanked Sammy for the gift and always saved a stool for him.

I didn't even tell Gootie that I had actually seen these spurts of ten-minute gambling in factories. That it went on in the barbershop she knew; Rocky told her. To avoid the gamblers he went to Tom Virzone's, a one-chair shop that didn't even have a candy-striped pole. The floors were dirty, and Virzone, the barber, when he wasn't working, sat in the elevated chair, chewed tobacco, and spat.

"Better than being with the gamblers," Rocky said. He wanted me to stay away from Winchell's barbershop; so did Gootie. "If you're with gamblers," she said, "you'll become one, too. Then you can forget about your store and your wife."

I risked getting my haircuts with gamblers, but the more I understood at the barbershop, the more dangerous gambling seemed. Every time I saw my father put a rubber band around three or four decks I didn't want to ride in the truck with him. I even asked him to stop playing poker.

"It's not gambling," he said. "It's recreation. A lot of the fellows go fishing or bowling—I don't care for that. But you can't beat a good poker game."

Because he made a living I thought we were safe from the fate of gamblers. "As long as he's got Kalkaska we'll be all right," Gootie said. "From Kalkaska he makes a living." We all understood the importance of Kalkaska. The scrap from that one factory, Gootie said, kept us from the poorhouse.

The Kalkaska Heater Company was my father's only major customer. It produced scrap every week, year round. His other customers, machine shops, small tool-and-die makers, and auto shops, needed only occasional scrap pickups. To us, Kalkaska, a tiny city in northern Michigan, was the most important place in America. Whenever someone from the heater factory came to Grand Rapids they had an open invitation to visit us, and they often did.

They were our guests of honor, but they were humble people, assembly-line workers, lift-truck drivers, loading-dock workers, the men who over the years had befriended my father.

To them, Grand Rapids was the big city. They came only when they had to—for doctoring or to do some big Christmas shopping, and if they had time, they liked to stop at Sammy's house to have one for the road.

They got a lot more. Gootie and Bashy cooked for days in advance. For these visitors the slipcovers came off the couch, my sisters' debate trophies moved to the dining room, and I was on constant call, in case a Kalkaska man requested the Gettysburg Address.

Sam did the main work, but making a living was everyone's responsibility. My father couldn't pay as much for scrap as the junkyards did; he had to make up in personal services what he couldn't pay in pennies per pound. He counted on friendship, on trust, and when the men from Kalkaska stopped by, he counted on his family. We were ready to be impressive.

Gootie supervised the menu—always fish followed by barley soup and then roasted chicken and two or three kinds of cake for dessert. And the visitor never left empty-handed. In addition to leftovers he got a bottle of Manischewitz wine, a jar of herring in wine sauce, and a loaf of bread baked by Rocky.

My sisters and I were embarrassed. We knew these men had stopped by just to say hello or have a cup of coffee—instead they had to sit for a full meal, and it didn't matter if it was dinnertime or midmorning. We were always ready.

Gootie liked to be introduced where she was standing in the kitchen so the Kalkaska men wouldn't notice her bad leg. She instructed Rocky to stay out of the way; Sam was doing business. They started with a bottle of Seagram's. My father put it on the table with two glasses. Nobody used ice or mixers. Some guests stayed all day and finished the bottle between bursts of eating. Gootie told me that Sam had to drink with them.

"A goy can't do business without a bottle," she said. "Everyone knows that. You can give him the best food, borscht and potatoes and roasted meat, and he'll still say, 'Where's the whiskey? There's no business without whiskey.'"

Gootie admired the way the men from northern Michigan dressed. Their checked flannel shirts and the occasional fur trim on the hoods of their hunting coats were marks of their importance. She had seen such men in Vilna and Odessa. "Look how far Sam has come in the world," she pointed out, "that men like this should come to visit him."

Our visitors were invariably veterans. In 1952 all healthy men were veterans. They left Kalkaska to fight the Nazis and the Japanese—and recently the Koreans; then they came home and didn't miss the rest of the world.

Because we were the only Jews these men spoke to, we had to speak for the Jews. When the Rosenbergs were arrested for selling the secrets of the atomic bomb, my father had to explain in Kalkaska that the rest of the Jews were innocent. In northern Michigan nobody had sympathy for Communists. We were battling them in the cold war and in Korea, and in the midst of that war came news that the Rosenbergs gave the bomb to Russia.

My sisters, on their debate team, were arguing the affirmative and the negative sides of the Rosenberg case. While I ate supper I did my homework and listened to quotations from Morton Sobell and David Greenglass. We talked about the Rosenbergs as much as we talked about the Detroit Tigers or the boy my sister Bailey was dating. Gootie knew what the Rosenbergs were like.

"They were all over Odessa," she said. "Almost every Jewish family had a Communist, but if you admitted it, they shot you right in the street." In an act of great daring, Gootie's mother once hid the son of one of their Odessa neighbors. "The soldiers were looking for him," Gootie said. "I was lying in bed with a big cast on my leg. Doctors in Sapitkin had put mud on my knee for weeks. Nothing helped—the TB got into the bone. I couldn't move. People who looked at me thought I'd never walk or even live through the winter. 'Put him here,' my mother said, 'in her room. They won't bother a sick person.'"

When the young man escaped he gave Gootie's mother a bushel of potatoes. "Communist, not a Communist, who cared?" Gootie said. "My mother helped a Jew because it's a mitzvah."

Rocky wanted the Rosenbergs hanged; my father tried to keep an open mind. When I listened to my sisters I felt swayed by both sides. I agreed with the affirmative and then with the negative.

"Leave it to Eisenhower," my father said. "He'll never let them electrocute innocent people."

While we waited for Eisenhower to decide the fate of the spies, Doug Bass came to visit. We only had a day's notice. He had never come alone before, always with his wife, Maureen. Doug counted more than anyone else. To others he was the head of maintenance; to us he ruled Kalkaska. One call from Doug could bring in a competitor to buy the scrap and change our lives.

"Don't worry about Doug," my father said, "he's like a brother." Doug had been coming over at least during deer season for as long as we could remember. He was no quick meal; Doug always threatened to stay for the whole bottle, but Maureen never allowed it. This time, without his wife, he announced his intentions.

"We'll kill the bottle, Sammy," he said. "We've got all day."

He had come to service his pickup and to buy wading boots for duck hunting. He brought in the boots to show us. Gootie had never seen such boots; none of us had. After a few drinks, Doug modeled them. They encased his legs to the groin. He stood at the dining table, made a rifle of his extended arm, and imagined himself waist deep in a swamp, shooting ducks from our ceiling.

"He's like a landlord," Gootie said. "They used to ride up on horses with big boots like that. They worked for the czar. People bowed down when they passed by."

In the dining room Doug squinted and pulled the imaginary trigger. Bashy carried out roasted chicken and potato pancakes.

"Just like that." Doug laughed. "I shoot a duck and it's out here dressed and cooked."

My father rolled up his sleeves. The men ate for an hour and worked on the bottle. Both their faces turned ruddy from the whiskey.

"You can't drive home," Bashy said. "Spend the night here."

"If I do"—Doug laughed—"Sammy'll put out another bottle and it'll be just as bad tomorrow."

In the kitchen, we worried. Bashy wanted to take Doug's keys so he couldn't drive home.

"You don't insult a man like him," Gootie said. "If he wants another car or truck, he snaps his fingers and people bring him one. You think this is the first time he's finished a bottle of whiskey? Even in Serei where there were no men like him, the peasants would come in, put all their money on the table, and say, 'Bring vodka, until all the money's gone.' Leave him alone," Gootie said. "He's a boss. If he wants to finish the bottle, don't get in his way."

Bashy sent in my sisters to distract the drinkers. While the girls argued the affirmative and the negative of the Rosenberg case I waited in the kitchen, ready to go next with Abe Lincoln's Gettysburg Address.

Doug looked around at the evidence of a family treating him royally. He seemed moved by both arguments, but his face hardened.

"You know I like you, Sammy, and all your family . . . but the Rosenbergs and Jews like that, I wouldn't even give 'em a trial."

My father didn't answer. Doug said we should use the bomb on China while we could.

"It would kill thousands of innocent people," my father said.

"They've got plenty of people over there," Doug said. "They're loaded with people, and thanks to those Rosenbergs they're gonna have a bomb of their own. I say use ours while we can."

In the kitchen I translated for Gootie.

"Another Hitler," she said.

"He's talking about killing Koreans and Chinese," I told her, "not Jews."

"Don't believe that," she said. "He's only trying to be polite."

Rocky, who had been in the living room watching the news while my father and Doug drank, came into the dining room to join the men.

"We oughta bomb the shit outta them," Doug said. "Kill every damn Communist starting with the Rosenbergs."

"You're right," Rocky said. "I hate the son of a bitches, too."

A coughing spasm kept him from continuing. Doug Bass handed Rocky his drink.

"Drink to that," Doug said, "and it will be good for what ails you."

Gootie made a face when I told her that in the other room

Rocky had joined the drinkers. She peeked through the kitchen door. Doug examined Rocky's black yarmulke. He took it off Rocky's head and put it on his own.

"How's it look?" he asked. He stood to view himself in the mirror and staggered. Rocky supported him.

"I like you people," Doug said. "I've had a hell of a time. If I lived here, I'd weigh four hundred pounds."

My mother filled a thermos bottle with coffee and put one extra bottle of Manischewitz wine in the gift package for Doug's wife.

"Are you sure you can drive?" my mother asked.

"Drive?" Doug said. "You don't have to drive anymore. I got automatic transmission. I just point."

He pulled on his green hunting coat, the hood lined with the rabbits he had skinned. In one hand he held his wading boots, in the other the paper sack filled with food and wine. My father, as drunk as Doug, walked his friend to the door. We all came to the hallway to say good-bye. We shivered as he opened the door.

"Hey," Doug said, "I forgot this beanie." He took off the yarmulke and tossed it to Rocky.

"If I wear that home, everyone'll think I'm a goddamn Jew," he said.

My father still had a smile on his face when he punched Doug. The big man fell against the door. He dropped the paper bag.

"Sam," he said, "what the hell's going on?"

He walked out the door, leaving behind the Manischewitz wine and the leftover gefilte fish wrapped in two layers of aluminum foil. He had a Chevy pickup with a trailer hitch and a gun rack. When the truck was new a year earlier, my father and I had gone for a ride in it.

My mother screamed. She ran out without her coat to stop him. "Doug," she yelled, "you forgot the fish and the wine. . . ."

The maintenance man didn't stop. He gunned his eight-cylinder engine. My mother walked into the house in tears. "We're ruined," she said.

Gootie brought out a cold rag for her daughter's forehead. "It's the whiskey," she said. "He didn't know what he was doing."

My father sat at the dining room table, looking at his hands. In the early twenties he'd made some money as a club fighter. He still loved boxing. He taught me how to jab and stay on my toes. When I was three he bought me boxing gloves. He took me to the Golden Gloves before I ever went to a movie. He closed his eyes.

In the morning my mother wouldn't speak to my father. When he came home from work she said, "Call Doug and apologize or you might as well sell the truck." My father refused.

We took sides. Rocky said my father was right to hit Doug. Gootie said only a drunkard and a gambler gives up making a living. "What difference does it make what he says?" she insisted. "And anyway, what did he say—'goddamn Jew.' In Serei everyone said it; here, too. Why did he have to be so surprised that an important goy would say 'goddamn Jew'?"

Bashy went to the china cabinet, collected whatever whiskey bottles she found, and threw them into the garbage.

Later Gootie took them out and hid them in her room. "If this had happened in Serei," she said, "there you really could starve— but in America nobody starves. You think my brothers would let us starve?"

My father didn't go to his Wednesday night poker game. Thursday he had no business at all. He asked me if I wanted to go shoot pool. He was waiting for me in his truck in front of school. We went downtown to Scotty's, where there were about a dozen tables. I had been there a few times and could play well enough to make contact on every shot, but not much more. My father could sometimes clear the table.

"I learned to play," he told me, "when I worked as a pinsetter in a bowling alley. When I wasn't racking pins I could shoot pool free." He tried to teach me, but I couldn't see the table the way he did or hit with a smooth cue stroke. Still, I felt like a man whenever he took me to Scotty's.

We were playing eight ball when I asked him if we would end up in the poorhouse.

"There are no poorhouses in Grand Rapids," he said. "Don't listen to Gootie. We'll be okay."

He didn't play as well as usual. When we left Scotty's we walked a few blocks down lower Monroe Avenue to the Weiss Brothers' Shoe Store. I asked if he couldn't go to the real boss, someone higher than Doug. He shook his head.

"You think Wilson, the boss, cares who picks up the scrap? He just wants the loading dock clean. The company is on the Detroit Stock Exchange; the president has his own airplane. I couldn't even get in to see him . . . and even if I could, what would I say?"

My father accepted his defeat. "I shouldn't have done it," he said. "I wish to God he had never come over, but I'm not going to apologize, not until he does."

At the shoe store he applied for a job. He had worked there for a few years in the 1940s, and one of his old friends, Milford Marlette, managed the downtown store. Milford's ears stuck out from his head and he wore oversize glasses and shirt collars a size bigger than his neck, but my father said that nobody knew shoes the way Milford did.

While Milford and my father talked I looked at the bones in my feet, outlined in green on the X-ray device that Milford used to insure a correct fit.

"I knew I could count on Milford," my father said. "If it comes down to it, I can always get my old job back."

"Shoes," my mother said. "You think you'll send three children to college selling shoes?"

Gootie said it had to happen. The drinking and gambling sooner or later had to lead to this or worse.

My father punched Doug on a Tuesday. On Saturday he announced that he wasn't even going to drive to Kalkaska on Monday. "Why waste the gas money?" he said. "All I'll have to do is turn around and come back."

He didn't want to be humiliated in front of his friends, the men from the heater factory who over the years had come to our house and had experiences not unlike Doug's, until the final seconds.

On Saturday night my mother called Doug's wife, Maureen, "just to say hello," she said. "She didn't mention anything," Bashy said. "We talked about recipes. She told me she's going duck hunting with Doug next month. I didn't know what to say. I asked her if Doug was all right. 'Better than ever,' she said."

We couldn't understand it. "Maybe she's afraid to tell you the truth," Gootie said. "He probably beats her, so she's afraid to say anything."

Saturday my father didn't go to the synagogue. Our house was quiet. My sisters didn't want to be at home; they went to see their friends. My father had never missed going to Kalkaska on a Monday unless it was Rosh Hashanah or Yom Kippur, and when that happened he went the day before. He had gone on freezing mornings even when he had the flu. The dock had to be clear of scrap for new deliveries. He never risked not doing his work the way he had to, and then in one drunken moment he threw it away.

Saturday night Gootie said she would call her brother Leo, "the millionaire." He owned a junkyard in Alma. "He'll give Sam a job," she said. "If we have to, we'll move to Alma."

"We're not moving to Alma," my father said. "We're not going anywhere. I made a living during the Depression; I'll make a living now."

Gootie didn't think Alma was so bad. "It's better than Odessa," she said. "In Odessa there were Jews who could be in shul in the morning and in jail in the afternoon—regular gangsters, pickpockets, thieves. While I was lying in bed wondering if I'd have one leg or two my father would come home and tell me what he'd seen. In Alma there are no criminals. The Jews and the goyim live in peace; everyone makes a living, and my brother Leo is like a king."

On Sunday night while we were watching *The Ed Sullivan Show*, my father stood up.

"I'm going to Kalkaska tomorrow," he said, "like always."

None of us could sleep that night. Rocky woke up at three, and I heard him. When my father left the house at five everyone but Gootie was awake to say good-bye. We watched him cross the street to the garage where he kept his truck, then we couldn't see anything until the red taillights of his Dodge backed out of the alley.

Rocky put on his coat and hurried out to give Sam one last chance to take him along.

"Go into Doug's office," Bashy said, "shake his hand and apologize. Remind him you have three children; he's a father, too."

"I'll do what I can," my father said.

"Don't be stubborn," Bashy said. "Tell him you were wrong."

"We both were," my father said.

"He doesn't have to know that," Bashy said.

I went to school Monday; then I came home to wait. It was well after dark before I heard the truck. My father parked in front of the house. He kept the motor running. I ran out to see him. Before he climbed out of the cab I could see the drums of brass and the steel clippings pushed tight at the back of the truck's body.

"A full load," my father said. He picked me up and kissed me.

In the house after he parked the truck, we all heard the story.

"Nothing," my father said. "It was like every Monday. I loaded the truck. Nobody stopped me. When I had the weight, I walked to Doug's office so he could sign the slip. 'How ya doin', Sammy?' he said, and he signed like nothing happened."

"Nothing did happen," Bashy said. "You were both drunk. Forget about it."

"You were lucky," Gootie said. "You hit a goy and didn't have to run away. Even Moses had to leave Egypt when he did that."

"It won't ever happen again," my father said.

"You can't be sure," Gootie said. "In America everything happens."

Chapter 12

*T*here was only one person in Grand Rapids who could study with Rocky. "No matter what Levinsky says," Gootie instructed us, "no matter what he does, try to agree with him. Without him there's nobody for Rocky." So when Levinsky came over every Saturday afternoon Gootie played the perfect hostess. Rocky's study partner never tired of praising himself.

"When I came to Michigan," he often said, "there were trees and lumberjacks. You couldn't find a Jew. I sent pictures of myself to Detroit and Chicago and Cleveland. You should have seen the letters I got back. Women from all over wanted to get on the train and come to Grand Rapids. 'I've never seen a face like that,' they wrote. 'The czar himself doesn't look so distinguished.' And what was I then? A peddler twenty years old and not worth fifty dollars including my horse and wagon. But quality is quality."

Levinsky's wife never interrupted her husband and never criticized him. "She's so afraid of him," Gootie said, "that she won't boil an egg without asking him if she can—and if he says yes, she'll still ask him for how long."

While the timid Mrs. Levinsky and Gootie waited downstairs, Rocky and Levinsky studied Talmud across the table from one another. Whenever I crept upstairs to watch, there was nothing to see.

Rocky moved his body back and forth rhythmically; Levinsky sat still. They both wore suits and ties and black yarmulkes. Levinsky had to squint through his glasses to see the small print. He was envious of Rocky's perfect vision. "Goodstein," Levinsky said, "without glasses you can see a bird shit at the end of the block, but you'll still step in it."

Rocky never took the bait. He let Levinsky tease him. Sometimes they argued over a phrase, but it was in Hebrew and I didn't understand what they argued about.

Rocky mumbled; Levinsky mumbled. They turned the pages. It was as if nothing happened. A few times I tried to join them, but Rocky had no patience. He read me a few lines from the Mishnah.

"God gave the Torah to Moses at Mount Sinai; Moses gave it to Joshua; Joshua passed it on to the elders. From the elders it went to the prophets; from the prophets to the men of the Great Assembly . . ." Rocky kept his finger on the page. I couldn't understand the Hebrew, but he translated to Yiddish for me.

"From one generation to the next," he said, "until you."

"What do you want from the boy?" Levinsky said. "Leave him alone. Nobody in this town knows anything. Why should he be different?"

"In Yagistov," Rocky said, "he would have known pages of the Mishnah by heart at his age."

Levinsky winked. "Tell your grampa where he is," he said. "Is this Yagistov?"

Levinsky always tired first. When he said, "Time for tea," they came downstairs.

I told Gootie that the Mishnah ended with me.

"Don't listen to him," she said. "You think you're the first person in the world who couldn't study? Look at my brothers. You think they're scholars? When there are nine men ready to daven, if all nine are wise men, what difference does it make? There's still not a minyan without a tenth. All nine of them can brag as much as Levinsky. They can know the Torah by heart, but each one counts exactly the same. One is one. Those nine scholars can't daven together, but let my brother Leo or you or any simple Jew walk in and right away there's a minyan.

"And you know what's just as important as studying? Charity. You'll have two stores and give to the poor, and if you do that, it's better than being a scholar."

"She's right," Levinsky said. "In Grand Rapids two stores is better than Torah—even one store is. We're living among fools. And the rabbis are no better."

Levinsky had helped to found the synagogue. He had been its first president. His photograph in a brown oval frame had been displayed prominently for thirty years next to the bronze tablets that held the names of the dead.

In the new synagogue structure, built without his approval, they moved his photo to the basement along with a line of the photos of other past presidents. "I did everything," he said, "and now they put me next to men who just come to a meeting and say, 'Meeting adjourned. Amen.'"

He complained to the board, but they refused to move his photograph. He stopped attending the synagogue.

"If they put me in the basement," he said, "I put them in the toilet."

When he tried to convince Rocky to join his boycott Gootie told him to lay off.

"You've got a business," Gootie said. "All he's got is *Shabbes.*"

After he retired Rocky started waiting for the Sabbath on Wednesday. By the time it actually arrived on Friday night he had been waiting for so long that all he wanted to do was speed through the ritual and get it over as quickly as possible. On Saturday morning he was at the synagogue by seven for a nine o'clock service.

Every year or two we needed a new rabbi; Grand Rapids seemed like a starter job, not a career. A succession of young clergymen had put up with Rocky, but in one young rabbi Rocky met his match. The new rabbi wanted the congregation to sit together in the front rows instead of having the fifteen or twenty Saturday morning regulars scattered throughout the two hundred seats in the sanctuary.

After weeks of asking everyone to move to the front, the rabbi, at his own expense, bought decorative white ropes to cordon off all but the first two rows. Every Saturday morning Rocky pulled the rope from his place, the last seat in the last row, and sat down to pray. When the rabbi spoke, Rocky used the time to recite out loud all the Hebrew prayers that the rabbi had intentionally omitted. Finally the rabbi couldn't take it any longer.

I read the rabbi's letter aloud to Gootie after Rocky had thrown it in the garbage. The young man had minced no words. He ordered Rocky to sit with everyone, to observe the decorum of the service, or else to stay home. "I work hard to prepare a sermon every week," he wrote. "Please be courteous enough to let me deliver it."

"For forty-nine years I've been sitting in my place," Rocky said, "in three different buildings. Let's see if he can move me."

When Rocky showed him the letter, Levinsky gloated. "You see," he said, "this is what they've wanted all along, to get rid of you. They didn't have to send me a letter. I knew it myself."

"Let him dare to throw me out," Rocky said.

"If he doesn't throw you out, someone else will," Levinsky said. "The shul is finished—over—I've been telling you for years. Now you've seen for yourself."

Gootie understood that Levinsky had something up his sleeve.

"Sure, they have a building," Levinsky said, "and across the street the bowling alley is also in a new building. For that rabbi and the people who hired him the bowling alley is also their shul. Every week they play bowling."

"Bingo," I corrected.

"It's all the same," Levinsky said, "a new building, games, raffles, women, dances. A shul is a place to study Torah—for that they have no time."

"If he tries to move me from my seat," Rocky said, "I'll break his arm."

"Then they'll put you in jail," Levinsky said, "or in a crazy house, and they'll keep on with their bowling and bingo. There's only one way to stop them and you know it. You've got a vacant house across the street," he said, "that's all we need. If I had a vacant house, I'd have started a shul two years ago."

"If all you need is a few rooms," Gootie said, "go ahead, rent an apartment, a better one than ours."

"If I did that," Levinsky said, "there would be expenses, upkeep. Pretty soon I'd be charging people to belong like those gangsters are doing. Anyway—I've tried—you know that. When I tell a landlord I'll be bringing people there—ten, twenty, maybe fifty—he wants to charge like for a mansion."

"I've told you a hundred times," Gootie said, "I'd give you the apartment for anything else, but not to destroy a shul."

"I'm not destroying anything," Levinsky yelled, his face becoming red. "It's already destroyed."

Rocky had wavered. As long as he was able to go to the synagogue and continue praying as he always had, he didn't join Levinsky's plan for a competing synagogue. With one letter the young rabbi made him change his mind.

Gootie was against a rebel movement to start another shul. "I don't think anybody will come to your shul," she told Levinsky, but she had another reason. For Gootie, the apartment Levinsky wanted was a haunted place. She didn't say that; nobody did, but we all knew it. Larry and his family lived downstairs and other tenants had before them, but nobody had used the upstairs since Max's death in 1937. For more than fifteen years the upper apartment remained empty. Gootie wouldn't talk about it when I asked her. My father explained it.

"She hasn't gone in there," he said, "since Max's funeral.

She'd rather lose money than go up there and think about his death all over again."

"But she talks about him anyway," I said, "all the time."

"It doesn't make sense," my father said, "but leave her alone. I wouldn't want her to go back to what it was like then, not for anything. If she wants to leave the apartment vacant, then it'll just be vacant."

I had been there a few times with Rocky, once to see if a pipe had broken when there was water downstairs, another time when Rocky noticed a flame at night and thought there might be a fire, but it was only Larry's boys with their Zippo lighters.

Rocky had no fear of the apartment. There were no taboos for him; still, he didn't contest leaving it empty.

Gootie gave Levinsky a flat no, even after Rocky joined the boycott of the synagogue.

"He'll change his mind," Gootie said. "All the rabbi has to do is call him up for an aliyah and give him a chance to donate money. He'll say, 'A hundred dollars in memory of my father,' and he'll feel like a big shot and forget he was ever mad at the rabbi. The problem will be the hundred dollars. Every time he gets mad at someone it's expensive."

She was wrong. This time Rocky stayed home. He didn't budge even when Gootie suggested that he go to make a donation. All summer he stayed home on Saturday mornings but kept his regular schedule. On Thursday he made the dough for challah and took a bath. On Friday morning, in his brown suit and red tie, he was all dressed up with nowhere to go. He spent the Sabbath alone and angry.

I went to the synagogue with my father. Rocky didn't try to stop us. I dozed through the sermon and skipped most of the prayers. Without Rocky swaying his body and making a lot of noise in the last row, it didn't feel like a synagogue to me. There were others who felt the same way. I heard Seymour Grossman, the president, ask my father if there was anything he could do to make Rocky return. When my father asked, Rocky gave his conditions—fire the rabbi and return the synagogue to Orthodoxy.

"I guess he'll just have to stay home, then," Seymour told my father. "Nobody can make the world go backwards for him."

When the High Holy Days approached, Rocky woke me one morning in an unusually gentle way. Instead of *yanek*, "farmer," he called me *mein kind*, "my child." I knew something was wrong.

He sat beside me on the bed. "I'm an old man," he said, "who knows how long I've got left. I've got no job and now no shul." His voice was soft, melancholy. "I'm trying to hold on until your bar mitzvah—but two years—I don't know."

"You'll be there," I said.

"In two years," he said, "you won't remember that you had a grampa."

"Don't say that," I said. "You know it's not true."

I had never heard him feel sorry for himself; it startled me. He pulled his light brown suitcase with straps from the closet. "I'm leaving," he said.

I jumped out of bed and tried to pull the suitcase back into the closet. It was heavy—he had already packed.

"You're not leaving," I said.

"I have to," he said. "I can't be without a shul."

I ran downstairs to alert everyone. My mother already knew and didn't seem alarmed. "He's going to Mount Clemens," she said. "It's near Detroit."

I was crying. "We can't let him go."

"Don't worry," Bashy said, "he'll be back right away."

"He told me he's leaving forever because there's no shul for him here."

"Don't listen to him," Bashy said. "He's being dramatic because you fall for it. He'll be back before you miss him."

When she woke up, Gootie had the same opinion. "Who will put up with him?" she said. "He'll be back in a few days. He didn't make any donations here, so he'll give all his money to the shul there and he won't even have bus fare home."

I knew they were wrong. I watched him count his money and fold a hundred dollars so that it fit into his zippered change purse.

His nephew Joe, a dentist in Detroit, had found him an inexpensive room. "Fifteen dollars a week," Rocky told me, "and once the woman who runs the rooming house sees what I can bake she'll probably stop charging rent if I work one day a week. And I'll look for a full-time job. Maybe in Mount Clemens they'll hire me."

He had me in tears. "I'll call you from Mount Clemens," he said. "Don't worry about me."

My father and I drove him to the Greyhound station. I walked onto the bus with him. He was a half hour early, the first one on the bus as soon as it was announced. He slid the suitcase under his feet, then put his arms around me. "Study for your bar mitzvah," he said, "but don't listen to anything that son of a bitch rabbi says."

"It's two years until my bar mitzvah."

"The time will go fast," he said, "you'll see."

The bus began to fill up. My father waited for me in the terminal. I could see him drinking coffee from a paper cup and reading the paper.

"Can I go with you?" I asked Rocky.

He shook his head. When I started to cry he said, "Maybe after the holidays. If I get a job, I'll rent a bigger room and then you can come."

I sat next to him until the driver took my hand and led me to the door. My father tried to comfort me.

"He's had fights with rabbis before," my father said. "He'll get it out of his system and he'll come home."

I knew I would never see Rocky again. His sweetness that morning had convinced me that he was saying good-bye forever. Without Rocky I couldn't sleep. I went into the living room and noticed the empty shelf in the bookcase. An entire row of his oversize books was gone. I realized why his suitcase had been so heavy.

I ran downstairs. Gootie was still awake, and she understood how serious the situation was.

"You're right," she said, "he wouldn't take the books if he was coming back."

With a shul and a job, Mount Clemens could keep him permanently. I would see him only once a year when we went to Detroit for a Tigers' game.

"I lived without him for twelve years when he left for America," Gootie said. "It wasn't so bad, except for the war."

I felt as if I were the only one who couldn't live without him. I waited for him to phone, but he didn't. He left just before the holiday season so he could spend Rosh Hashanah and Yom Kippur in an Orthodox synagogue.

I hoped he might come back the day after Yom Kippur. When he didn't return, my mother called Rocky's nephew in Detroit to find out where in Mount Clemens Rocky had been staying for three weeks.

"I haven't seen him," his nephew said, "and he hasn't called." He looked through the Mount Clemens phone book for us and came up with a list of rooming houses near the synagogue. Bashy called them. Nobody had seen a five-foot-tall man in a brown suit and a cap who might be looking for work in a bakery.

My mother still didn't worry. "He probably decided to stay until after Sukkos," she said. "He's there—maybe someone he met in shul is letting him stay at their house."

I thought he was dead.

"No," Gootie said. "God forbid, if he was dead, you'd hear right away."

While we waited to hear from Rocky we looked for a new house.

"When he comes back," Gootie said, "we'll tell him we're moving. He won't have to walk so far; you'll see it will make a big difference."

Ever since the synagogue moved to its new building at the top of Michigan Hill Gootie had been talking about moving. During the winter the three-mile uphill walk took a lot out of Rocky. He wouldn't ride on the Sabbath.

On Sundays she and I spent hours with the newspapers as I read her the real estate want ads. She thought most of the ads were fakes. "Nobody wants to sell a good house," she said. "If they're selling, either someone died there and they have to leave like we did, or else the house is cursed."

We read the ads for weeks before I dared to call a realtor. Gootie was as nervous as I was. She'd bought the house we lived in and Dorothy's, across the street, by direct negotiation, in Polish, with the owner. A real estate agent sounded to her like a government official.

I would read the small print on the page—something like "three bedrooms, one bath, linoleum floors, gas heat"—and Gootie would fill in the rest. She made stories out of real estate language. A linoleum floor might mean that the wife thought a lot of herself: she entertained; she belonged to ladies' clubs; she probably had a fur coat. The woman must be like her brother Leo's daughter, who changed her name from Rose to Roz so people would think she was a Yankee. Her husband went along, put in the linoleum floor himself after he came home from work. And then it still wasn't good enough for her. She nagged and nagged; the husband got angry. One night he broke the dishes, slammed the door, and stayed out all night. In the morning the wife called the real estate lady and told her about the linoleum flooring. A house like that we didn't even want to look at.

But there were houses that sounded too good to miss—duplexes, triplexes, houses that you could live in while the tenants paid all the expenses.

"I'm calling for my grandmother," I told Mrs. Ellis of Albert Realtors. "She has ten thousand dollars cash."

Mrs. Ellis picked us up the following Sunday afternoon in a 1951 Olds 88. She helped Gootie into the backseat.

"Tank you," Gootie said. In her purse she carried the Old Kent bankbook, but Mrs. Ellis never asked to see it. She drove us all over the Hill District. Gootie told me to offer her a dollar for gas, but the real estate lady refused to accept it.

"It's my job," she said.

Gootie whispered in my ear that we were lucky we had found a crazy lady with nothing to do.

Mrs. Ellis called us every time there was a new listing near the synagogue. The longer Rocky stayed away, the more halfhearted Gootie and I felt about moving. By the end of Sukkos, the next major holiday, my mother was ready to call the state police. We hadn't heard from him in six weeks. Bashy called every bakery in Mount Clemens again, then we called everyone he knew in Detroit.

Gootie said it was possible that devils had kidnapped him. "He's not afraid of anything; maybe one night he had no place to stay so he slept in a shul. Because there are no mezuzahs on the door of a shul any devil can go in, and you know him—if he saw a devil, he wouldn't run away."

One day, when Mrs. Ellis called with a new listing, I told her the truth. "We don't need a house," I said. "My grampa's gone."

"I'm so sorry," she said. The following day she sent flowers.

In late October, almost two months after he boarded the Greyhound, Rocky called home.

"We've been worried sick," Bashy said. "We've called everyone in Mount Clemens."

"Mount Clemens," Rocky said. "If I'd stay in Mount Clemens, I might as well stay home. The shul there is almost as bad."

"Where are you?" Bashy asked.

"I'm in South Haven," he said, "and I'm happy."

The following Sunday my parents, Gootie, and I drove to South Haven. Only an hour and a half from Grand Rapids, South Haven sat on the shore of Lake Michigan, directly across from Chicago.

It was not a popular beach town for Michigan people, but at one time it had drawn a Chicago crowd, including observant Jews, and even a generation after its heyday there was still a small synagogue and a kosher boardinghouse.

Rocky slept in a room barely big enough for a bed, and he was helping the landlady in the kitchen. The bathroom was down the hall. He shared a parlor, too, with three Chicago men who were staying until Mrs. Finklestein closed her boardinghouse for the winter. When we arrived, I didn't leave his side.

He wouldn't come home with us—he had enough money to

stay another month—but at least we knew where he was, and we had the telephone number of the pay phone in the hallway. The next day, after school, Gootie asked me to walk with her to Levinsky's house.

"It's a terrible sin," she said, "to destroy a Jewish community, but with a husband like this what can I do? He'll come home when they close the rooming house for the winter, but next year he'll do this all over again. We have to start a new shul."

She told Levinsky he could have the apartment. "It's just an apartment," she said, "four rooms filled with my sorrow. How are you going to make a shul there?"

"You'll see," Levinsky said. "Now that we'll have a place, you'll see."

"You'll need a Torah," Gootie said. "You can't have a shul without a Torah."

"I'll look into it," Levinsky said.

"You'll look," Gootie said. "That I know, but will you put up any money?"

Levinsky smiled. "I'm not going to argue with you, or you might take back the apartment."

"I gave the apartment," Gootie said, "now you give a Torah."

"Leave it to me," Levinsky said. "Don't forget I've started a shul before."

"If I leave it to you," Gootie said, "we'll have a Torah when the Messiah comes and gives you one free of charge."

Chapter 13

When we drove to Alma the following Sunday, everyone else in the family thought it was just one of our usual trips to visit Gootie's youngest brother, Leo, and his wife, Yachey. I knew we were going for a Torah.

Leo and Yachey had married in Serei before World War I and then emigrated immediately to America. Forty years later they still had marital problems. Gootie served as their counselor. She loved her brother, but she always took Yachey's side.

Yachey said there were other women.

Gootie tried to soothe her. "How could he look at other women?" Gootie said. "You're more beautiful than anyone."

She was. At sixty Yachey's round face seemed unlined. She bought her clothes in Detroit and had her hair and nails done in a beauty shop.

"He doesn't look at me," Yachey said. "He goes to restaurants, to movie houses. I know. People tell me what he does."

Gootie urged patience. "He's already old," she reminded Yachey. "A man his age doesn't look for other women."

"He's strong as an ox," Yachey said. "He's strong enough for ten women."

"He's a good man," Gootie insisted, "but the money has gone to his head."

Yachey lived on the first floor of their brick ranch house on Alma's main street, right across from Alma College. Leo lived in the finished basement.

They greeted us separately, Yachey at the front sun porch, Leo near the basement stairs. The men, my father and I, visited Leo first, while Bashy, Gootie, and my sisters visited Yachey. Later we switched floors.

Leo had one gold front tooth and most of his hair. He had the physique of a forty-year-old. My father liked him. They had the scrap business in common, but Leo's was a vast enterprise. He controlled the steel market in central Michigan. His trucks roamed between Bay City and Saginaw and as far away as Lansing. He owned a machine that could crush a car in seconds and had dozens of employees, but he still did hard physical labor himself. His hands were callused and even on Sunday showed bits of grease around his nails.

While the women talked upstairs, Leo and my father had a drink at Leo's well-stocked bar. In addition to his Johnnie Walker Scotch Leo had a bed, a TV, a small kitchen, and a Ping-Pong table that he had set up for his grandchildren. Upstairs Yachey had all four bedrooms, an enclosed sun porch, and two freezers filled with kosher meat shipped directly to her by the Boxman Brothers' Butcher Shop in Detroit. She kept a large bowl on her windowsill filled with the steel kosher marking tags she removed from her frozen chickens. She held the bowl in front of me as if it contained candy or baseball cards.

"Look," she said, "I check every time." In the drawers of her French provincial desk she showed me thank-you letters from many charities.

"Poor people all over the world love me."

Yachey said everything that came to her mind and in whatever order the thoughts arrived. Her English shaded into Yiddish as soon as she got excited, then went back and forth, sometimes word by word.

Her neighbors in Alma couldn't understand her linguistic mix, and Leo didn't try. Wrapped in mink, she roamed her big house, imagining her husband's liaisons and the life she might have had in Serei or even Grand Rapids. Her sons and her daughter had little patience. Only Gootie sympathized.

"He did it to her," Gootie said. "He made her move to Alma with four children and nobody to talk to."

"The woman has everything in the world," Leo said. "She doesn't like Alma, I bought her a house in Florida. Go ask her why she won't go there. She's got a car, but she won't learn to drive."

Yachey cursed him using the words for cholera, leprosy, a fire in his intestines, and boils, but she added a negative before each curse. She used the Yiddish diminutive of his name. "Lashky, he treats me so badly, he shouldn't get the worst cholera in the world, boils shouldn't cover him from head to foot."

By the time Gootie had listened to Yachey's complaints and made her way slowly down the basement stairs, Leo had already had a few drinks. He hugged her. Their faces were similar, but Leo, almost six feet tall, towered over his sister. He deferred to Gootie, understood that her role was to chastise him for ignoring his wife.

"Leo," Gootie said, "you don't live like a Jew."

He laughed his big laugh. "I guess I don't," he said.

"You have a hard life."

He laughed again. "If you say so. What's she been telling you upstairs?"

"You know what she tells me."

"She tells everybody," Leo said, "and some people even understand. I went into the A and P last week and the cashier said to me, 'I hear you've taken up with another woman.'"

"She's lonely," Gootie said.

"She should go to Florida," Leo said. "She can talk all day there."

"She wants you to go with her," Gootie said.

"I've got a business. I can't just run away. And she'd drive me crazy. There's no basement in the Florida house."

"Your troubles," Gootie said, "I wouldn't wish on my worst enemy. But as long as you're healthy."

Then she brought up her subject. "There's a way," Gootie said, "to make up for some of what you've done."

"What have I done?" Leo said. "I work all day, I take a shower, and I go to bed."

"God sees everything," Gootie said.

Leo laughed. "That's okay with me," he said.

"What do you have here?" Gootie asked.

Leo looked around his well-stocked basement. "Everything," he said.

"Is there a Jewish book in your house, a prayer book?"

"She's got all kinds of prayer books upstairs. Anybody that rings the doorbell, she gives them five dollars. She's got Mormon books, Seventh Day Adventist—she doesn't know the difference." He laughed again. "I don't either."

"It's not a joke," Gootie said. "You've lived like this most of your life. You have money, but what else?"

Leo thought about it.

"I don't worry about things like that. I go to work; I come home. She doesn't want me in the house, I'll stay down here until I die."

He laughed again.

"What about your sins?" Gootie said. "Don't you think about your sins?"

"No," Leo said, "I don't. I've got other things on my mind."

"God gives everyone a chance to repent," Gootie said, "no matter what they've done."

"I haven't done anything."

"Liar," Yachey called out from the top of the stairs. "Everybody saw you with Mrs. Evans, who should be ashamed, a grandma herself and with orange makeup that makes her look like a pumpkin."

"That's what she tells people," Leo said. He shrugged. "I don't care anymore. She can say whatever she wants."

Gootie urged Yachey to shut the door and return to the kitchen.

"Everybody sins," she reminded her brother, "but not everybody has a chance to buy a Torah."

Leo looked at her.

"That's right, you've got a chance now."

"A Torah," Leo said loudly; then he almost doubled over in laughter.

"You see," Yachey yelled down, "for God he gives nothing. He wouldn't give me anything, either, but he knows I can tell the government that he doesn't pay enough taxes. I've got the government's telephone number, and I'll tell them about Mrs. Evans too and he'll pay double. Nobody can believe it, a man with a business like his and grandchildren. You think I don't cook every day? Chicken, steaks, in the barbecue like on the television, and he stays in the basement and eats from cans or at the Big Boy. He bought the Big Boy. I know—Ben told me he bought the Big Boy and I'll tell the government that, too."

"Why do I need a Torah?" Leo asked.

"I need it," Gootie said. She told him about the synagogue we were going to start in the apartment across the street from our house. "I want a Torah, and I want it donated in memory of Max. The shul will be right in the living room where he used to listen to the radio."

"How much does a Torah cost?"

"Ten thousand dollars," Gootie said.

Leo let out a whistle. "What about Levinsky?" he said. He remembered Levinsky from his years in Grand Rapids. "Levinsky's loaded."

"You know he doesn't give a penny for anything."

"Then why should I buy a Torah for him?" Leo said. "If he wants a shul, let him buy his own Torah."

"Buy a Torah," Gootie said, "so that people will know that even though you live like this you haven't forgotten that you're a Jew."

Leo walked outside to think it over.

"If he doesn't buy one," I told Gootie, "we can buy one with the ten thousand dollars you have in the Old Kent Bank."

Gootie looked at me angrily. "Ten thousand dollars," she said, "isn't always ten thousand dollars."

I didn't understand.

"Ten thousand dollars is just a big number; it means a lot of money, that's all. You saw with the houses—they can say this house cost nineteen thousand, but when it's sold it can sell for ten thousand. Numbers don't mean anything. There's a lot of money like Leo has, and there's a little money like we have. Our ten thousand isn't like his ten thousand dollars. Ours comes from saving a dollar here, a dollar there. His comes from big trucks, from a junkyard, from banks; it's not the same kind of money."

We waited in the basement. Leo didn't return. "You see what he's like," Yachey told us upstairs, "he goes away to the women. Leprosy shouldn't cover him, and he shouldn't die of the worst cholera. You see what he's like. Don't worry, I'll tell the government about this, too."

On the ride home the disappointment in her brother made Gootie's motion sickness worse. In Lakeview, halfway between Alma and Grand Rapids, she had to suck on a lemon. We bought ice and put a cold compress on her head.

"All for nothing," she said. She didn't tell Levinsky about our failed trip.

The week after our visit to Alma, Leo and Yachey arrived unannounced. She carried two suitcases and a hatbox. Leo had done some investigating. The big amount of money that Gootie called $10,000 turned out to be $1,800. Leo added $200 for prayer books. He gave us the address of the synagogue in Chicago where the prepaid Torah awaited its new home.

"Rocky can go pick it up," he said.

We lined up to thank Leo for the Torah.

"It's me who's really buying it," Yachey said. "He told me that if I'd stay a week at Gootie's house, he'd buy the Torah."

"She's right," Leo said. He laughed and shook hands all around. "Whatever she says, she's right."

"You think I don't know why he wants me out of the way—I know, and I told the neighbors to watch."

My sisters moved into Gootie's room and gave Yachey the biggest room in the house. She said it was too cold and had no private bath. The noise we all made gave her a headache. Instead of the great lawn of Alma College she had to look out at Larry Hayes and his brood.

"I always suffer," she told Gootie, "and he gets the credit."

"This time," Gootie assured her, "your suffering is for a good cause."

"My name should be on the Torah, too," Yachey said.

"Of course," Gootie assured her. "Without you, Leo wouldn't be anything."

"You're the only one who understands that," Yachey said.

For a week the sisters-in-law huddled around the kitchen table. With a sympathetic audience Yachey complained less. She took off her mink jacket and left her frozen shoulder bare in the afternoons. She called Leo every day. At the shop he answered; at home he didn't.

"Don't worry," Gootie said, "he's in the basement—he knows it's you calling. He's not answering on purpose."

"He knows how to torture me," Yachey said. "If only I knew how to torture him."

Chapter 14

When Rocky returned from South Haven he put his books back in the bookcase and promised me that he'd never leave again. "I won't have to," he said. "We'll have such a good shul that people from South Haven will come to us." The new shul made him act like a new man. He took the bus to Chicago to pick up the Torah, but after a twelve-hour ride he returned empty-handed.

Gootie was furious. "I should have known better," she said. "I should have let someone else go or asked them to mail the Torah."

We were all disappointed. Levinsky had canvassed the west side of Grand Rapids, personally recruiting among the few Jews who still lived in the industrial neighborhood. He wanted to be sure that on Saturday the Torah would be greeted by the ten men needed to read from it. He was angry at Rocky, too. "You should have brought it," he said. "We could have worried about the problems later."

Rocky refused to back down. "That Torah had mistakes," he said. "Some of the letters were so faded you could barely see them."

"If there's a good reader," Gootie insisted, "he'd see the words. My brother buys you a Torah and it's not good enough. Did Moses send his Torah back?"

"He didn't get it from your brother," Rocky said. However, he was disappointed, too. "I don't know where he found that Torah; it hadn't been in a synagogue for years. It needs to be corrected and checked over, every word has to be right. I got someone to do it."

"Who do you know in Chicago?" Gootie asked.

"Rabbi Schwartz," Rocky said. "I met him in South Haven. He lived in the rooming house. For three hundred dollars he'll fix every mistake."

"You went to pick up the Torah and instead you found someone to take three hundred dollars from my brother."

"Who needs your brother?" Rocky said. "I told Rabbi Schwartz to check the Torah. I'll pay him."

"With what?" Gootie said. "You gave away all your money in South Haven. You don't have three hundred pennies."

"If your brother knew anything," Rocky said, "he would have paid three hundred dollars more and bought a Torah that had already been checked."

When Gootie asked Leo for the extra three hundred dollars he refused. "I bought a first-class Torah," he said. "If it was good enough for a shul in Chicago, it's good enough for Rocky and Levinsky. I won't pay someone three hundred dollars to rub shoe polish on a few letters."

Levinsky agreed. He wouldn't pay the correction fee, either. Without the Torah the new shul was stillborn.

On Saturday mornings Rocky and Levinsky went to the apartment and sat at opposite ends of the big table. They paid no attention to one another. Rocky sped through the service, then hurried outside to chase away the neighborhood kids who had gathered to see what the two old men in suits and funny hats were up to.

While our Torah was being corrected in Chicago, something else was scheduled there. Chuck Davy, our local boy, would be in Chicago to fight Chico Vejar, the number one contender. The winner would be guaranteed a shot at Kid Gavilan, the Havana bolo puncher, king of the welterweights.

At Winchell's barbershop a month in advance the men were betting on Davy. Hal and his son Vic, who cut at the second chair, had been following Davy since his amateur days.

"There must be a lot of people in Mexico or someplace down there who think a lot of their Chico," Hal Winchell reported, "because we're getting three to one on Davy, and they'll take as much action as we want."

I decided that the fight was a giveaway, not a gamble. I was ready to risk the poorhouse. "Bet everything," I told my father. "Chuck will kill him."

Most of the men in the shop agreed. Hal's contact in Chicago told him that more money was going on Davy from our location than from anywhere outside Detroit. "We're putting our money where our mouth is," Hal said, "but I'm worried because Chuckie couldn't knock out a nun, and you can't be sure Chico will let him dance around for ten rounds."

At home I practiced leading with my right, like Chuck, and backpedaling. I crouched and bobbed; I didn't sit still even when I talked to Gootie.

"You're making me sick," she said, looking away as I pretended the six-cubic-foot Westinghouse refrigerator was Chico Vejar.

"If it's a dance," I told her, "it's in the bag." I liked sounding knowledgeable, like the men in the barbershop, but boxing terminology didn't interest her in Yiddish or English.

Rocky watched the Wednesday night fights with us but disapproved of the Gillette fights from Madison Square Garden because they took place on Friday night.

About a week before the Davy fight, Hal, the barber, called

us. My father put the phone down. He asked my mother first. She shook her head. They argued; then he came into the dining room where I sat at his desk, reading a baseball book. "How would you like to see the Davy fight?"

"It's on TV," I said. "You know I won't miss it."

"I mean in person," he said. "Hal can get us tickets from his contact in Chicago. Your mother doesn't think you should go; you'll have to miss a day of school. I told him we'd take the tickets," my father said. He was as happy as I was.

All that week I thought of nothing but the fight, yet the word "Chicago" was loaded. There the corrected Torah sat awaiting three hundred dollars and a ride home. Gootie told me not to go anywhere with the gamblers.

She had heard about a man in Serei, a wagon driver, an honest man who never gambled. Once one of his passengers pulled out a pair of dice. While he was driving he lost the horse and the wagon. That story could have scared me away from a poker game, but not from a Chuck Davy fight.

My father understood what it meant for us to go to Chicago. He let me in on his secret.

"Of course I want to see the fight," he said, "and I want you to see it, but I decided weeks ago that I would have to pick up the Torah. We can't just let it sit there. Every Saturday when I see Rocky staying home while we go to shul, I know we've got to make sure he has his shul across the street."

When we told Hal, who was driving his Buick, that we wanted to stop on the west side of Chicago to pick up a Torah scroll, first he thought we were kidding. My father tried to explain.

"It's no problem," Hal said. "When I was a kid my dad would go ten miles out of his way, by horse and buggy, to get just the right Christmas tree."

Hal had a stop of his own to make. He would be wearing his money belt. We left at five A.M. and I slept most of the way. When I woke up, Vic had a map of Chicago in his lap. They decided that it made more sense to make their stop first.

While I slept they seemed to have discussed making more bets on the fight.

"I don't know," Hal said. "Usually I'm with the odds, but this time I guess I let my heart get to me—I really like Chuckie. If he loses, about six months of haircuts goes down with him."

Vic laughed. "And everything I've got saved for a new outboard motor."

"What the hell," Hal said. "How many times in your life do you get a chance to put money on a guy who lives up the road and probably has the best jab since Willy Pep?"

As we wound through the Chicago streets, Vic, who now carried the money, double-checked to make sure the doors were locked. "At home," he said, "I could leave it all in the cash register with the drawer wide open, but Chicago makes me nervous."

"Me too," my father said. "I've got the three hundred dollars in my front pocket."

"You've got about five more minutes," Hal said, "to put it down on Chuckie, at better than three to one. You could come home with a grand."

We had already bet ten dollars on Chuck, on the day we read about the fight. Five and ten dollars was all my father ever bet on any game or boxing match, but this was different.

"Bet it on Chuck," I said quietly to my father, but Vic and Hal heard.

"The boy's got nerve, Sammy," Hal said. "Think about it. When's the last time you looked at three to one on a bet you'd make even up?"

"That's true," Sam said. "I'd bet on Chuck without the odds."

"It's like a big sale at a store," Vic said, "or getting equipment wholesale. You can't really pass it up."

"It means a lot to the old man," my father said. "I don't want to risk it."

"It's your money," Vic said, "not Rocky's."

"The only guy I would never bet against," Hal said, "is Rocky. Imagine what he might have been like in the ring—what would he have been? A flyweight?"

My father had removed three hundred dollars from his savings account. "It's a month's work," he said.

"Twenty minutes for Chuckie," Hal said. "That's all it will take. I don't think Vejar can go better than six rounds. He cuts around the eyes, and you can bet that's where Chuckie's right is going to live. Six rounds and they'll stop it."

"Hal's right," I said. The excitement of actually being in Chicago for the fight was getting to me. "I'd bet everything if it were up to me," I said.

My father thought about it. "I did that once," he said. "I put everything on the '27 Pirates in the series and they lost. That's why I moved to Michigan."

"Baseball is too hard to figure," Hal said. "There's nine men and the bullpen and the weather. I'd never load up on baseball like I'd load up on a good fighter."

When we found the place they were looking for, Vic turned to the backseat.

"Last chance, Sam. If you don't want to put it all down—maybe another hundred on Chuck."

"I need the whole three hundred dollars," Sam said.

"Your call." Vic had his hand on the door. I held my breath. My father shook his head.

An hour later we had the Torah. My father wrapped it in a blue cotton blanket and placed it gently in Hal's trunk. We paid two dollars to park in a lot so the Torah would be in a guarded car.

All through the fight I watched Chuck's quick right hand do exactly what Hal said it would. I loved the words I heard in the crowd. "Double up on him, baby!" a man behind me kept yelling. I didn't know if he was rooting for Davy or Vejar. Everyone raved about Chuck's footwork and his jab. In person I could see the beads of sweat that flew off the fighters' bodies whenever a good punch landed. On TV I couldn't tell how hard the punches were. In person I could almost feel it every time Chuck took a solid right.

The fight went ten rounds, and Chuck won going away on all three scorecards. I slept all the way home with my head on my father's lap. At school nobody believed that I had really been at the fight.

Rocky carried the Torah across the street and put it on the big table in the living room. Levinsky held on to one side of the scroll as Rocky unrolled the parchment to check on the corrections. When he was satisfied he came back to tell us.

"Now it's a real Torah," he said. "Now we've got a shul."

Nobody seemed to ask where the three hundred dollars had come from, but the next week when I heard Gootie complain under her breath when my father left for his Tuesday night poker game, I stopped her.

"He's not a gambler," I said. After Chicago, I never doubted him again.

Chapter 15

*T*he shul started slowly. On its first Saturday morning when my father and I crossed the street at nine, the house looked the way it did on any other day. Larry perched in his ragged lawn chair, and a half dozen kids played on the sidewalk and in the alley beside the house.

"They're already praying up there," Larry told us, "and I'm keeping the kids quiet to get on the good side of Rocky."

Upstairs in the new house of worship the Torah lay on the big table and Rocky and Levinsky had been joined by Meyer Dribben, the glazier who had repaired the windows. He was not a religious man, but for the occasion he had removed the denim overalls he always wore. Dressed in a blue suit and a snap-brim fedora, he looked almost as dapper as Levinsky. Rocky wore his brown suit, and my father and I also wore suits. Although I wouldn't count toward the minyan until thirteen, I wanted to be there for the inaugural Sabbath.

My father didn't. "I'll help them out to start," he said, "but this isn't for me."

"Wait," Levinsky said, "people are coming. Everyone from the west side will be here, you'll see."

By ten, two retired furniture factory workers had raised our number to five eligible males—still five short of the quorum.

"They promised me," Levinsky said. He began to recite names. "They promised me. Next time I'll have them put it in writing."

Rocky didn't wait. He sped through the prayers and was ready to go home. "What good will writing do?" he said. "If they're liars, we don't need them."

"If I write it down and they sign, then they'll know I won't forget," Levinsky said. "They'll know God won't forget."

We were still at five when I saw, out the window, Gootie crossing the street. She was wearing her lace-up shoes, a dark gray dress, and a hat. I hadn't known she was coming. Larry took her arm as soon as she stepped up on the curb. Over Rocky's Hebrew mumbling of the prayers I could hear Larry and Gootie as he held her arm on the steep staircase.

"I didn't know you prayed, too," Larry said. "I thought only Rocky did that."

Gootie answered him with a Slavic phrase that she often used when she climbed stairs: "*Yedem shtevel droog-y-boot.*" It meant something like "One step at a time."

Larry laughed. "You might as well talk Yid talk. The only Polish word I know is *piva.*"

When they reached the top of the stairs I hurried over to escort Gootie into the apartment. I didn't want to give Rocky a chance to yell at Larry.

"Tank you," Gootie said.

"It's okay, missus," Larry said. "If all landladies were like you, I'd never have been evicted from anyplace."

"Tell him," Gootie said, "that he can live in the house a hundred years. He's a drunkard, but not a liar."

It embarrassed me to translate, but Larry didn't seem to mind.

We walked into the room in which Gootie had last seen her son alive. I heard the details many times—how Max combed his hair, put on his coat, then walked down this very staircase, stepped into his black Chevy, and drove off. I knew what Gootie was thinking. The box lined with blue cloth that Rocky had made for the Torah suddenly looked like a coffin.

She counted the men. "Just five," she said, shaking her head. She walked to the back of the room. Levinsky had brought a section of steel wire that he'd found in his junkyard to separate the men from the women. Gootie sat behind it, as alone in the women's section as if she were in prison.

"Let's go home," Rocky said to everyone. "Maybe next week we'll have a minyan."

"Wait ten more minutes," Levinsky said. "What's the hurry?"

A sixth man came up the stairs, Alter Schneiderman. Like Rocky and Levinsky, he was a man nearing eighty who still worked. He counted, too. "Six," he said, "no minyan, but enough for a good kiddush."

"That's all you care about," Rocky said. "You don't want a shul. You want a restaurant."

"Why not?" Schneiderman said. "God doesn't want people to starve."

From behind the steel wire Gootie invited Schneiderman to our house for lunch. He was a bachelor and lived in a single room. After the landlady with whom he had boarded for a generation died, he needed a place to eat on weekends.

Levinsky ignored the kiddush squabble. "Next week," he said, "we'll have ten, I promise. Don't forget I've been president of a shul before. I know what to do."

When the men shook hands and left I waited for Gootie. Her stiff leg was not the only thing that made her slow. She looked at everything for a long time, the way people in museums stand in front of paintings. There was always more to see in even the most ordinary scene, and this apartment turned shul was no ordinary scene. While the men stood out front discussing their strategy for finding more shul-goers the next week, Gootie stared at what had once been her kitchen. Electric cords taped at the end hung from a jagged hole in the plaster. She walked to a clean square spot on the linoleum. "Here was where we kept the icebox," she said. I knew she would be in a reverie and I didn't want to hear it, but I couldn't stop her. I hoped someone else would come up to interrupt her stream of memories.

She didn't say anything as she looked around the kitchen and the living room. Then she looked into the small, empty room. Rocky and Levinsky had stored cleaning materials in the kitchen. They had put the extra paint and folding chairs in one bedroom, and of course the Torah, the prayer books, and about fifteen folding chairs were in the living room. I knew what the empty room meant.

"He had a radio," Gootie said. "In those days who had a radio? And the golf clubs. He made money carrying golf clubs, and they taught him how to play. He used to tell me that he'd take me to golf someday to show me how beautiful the grass was . . . a store and a car and a radio. . . . He looked so good," she said, "when he left for the wedding. He had cream on his hair, and the waves stayed in place. In a year or two he would have gotten married himself. He was waiting for the store to get established."

Across the street, when Gootie talked about her son he seemed remote; here in the room he had actually lived in, I felt my uncle directly, even more than at the cemetery.

"People think and God laughs," Gootie said, trying to comfort herself with the proverb. I knew what I meant to her. I knew why she'd forbade me to drink cold milk in the morning, why she insisted that I wear a sheepskin coat and a hat to cover my ears from the wind. I knew why she watched me through the window all the time even though I was only a few feet away in the yard. But no matter how much I was watched and guarded, protected and loved, I was still me, my parents' Max, not hers, the replacement, not the real thing. I had not played in the snow in Odessa or milked cows in Serei. I had been born long after the peak of her grief but in the midst of the melancholy she never lost.

When her Max died, all the pleasure went out of Gootie's life, but the humor remained. Everything could be funny, but no amount of fun erased her sadness. Isolated from her new country by lack of English and from the community by staying at home, Gootie made an art out of being an outsider.

She touched the Torah, straightening its cover as if it were a child who had buttoned a sweater in the wrong holes. Six men, a boy, and an old woman, we were not enough to count as a prayer group and hardly a threat to the two-hundred-family Conservative synagogue, yet Rocky's shul had done a big thing: it brought Gootie back to a place she hadn't been able to face. She traced Max's name where Mrs. Duess, the seamstress, had sewed it onto the Torah cover. In a corner of the fabric, tucked against the parchment, her son's name must have seemed more permanent than his life.

"A Torah," Gootie said, "in his memory."

Chapter 16

*L*evinsky didn't lose confidence. "I'm stubborn," he said.

"Everyone from Minsk is stubborn," Gootie said. "You can hear Minsk in Levinsky's voice. They all think they're as strong as Samson and as wise as King Solomon. In Serei we wouldn't do business with someone from Minsk, but here . . ."

Between them Rocky and Levinsky could recall every Jew who had lived in Grand Rapids from 1900 to 1950. Even the ones who never came to the synagogue bought their bread at the American Bakery, and Levinsky, who had presided over the initial synagogue for years, made it his business to welcome strangers.

Like Rocky, he had never learned to drive. Every day after work he walked through the neighborhood, recruiting men for the shul. On the second Saturday he succeeded. There were six returnees plus a blind man, Mr. Bookholder, led by his wife, and a reluctant Jack Remes, the pharmacist at the corner Rexall store. Rocky had confronted him in his store.

"We need a minyan," Rocky said.

"I can't help you," Jack said. "What if a sick person comes in and needs medicine?"

"If he can come to your store," Rocky said, "he's not so sick. He can wait."

"It's against the law," Jack said. "A pharmacist has to be on duty."

"The law," Rocky reminded him, "says that a Jew has to go to shul on *Shabbes*."

Jack, in his white pharmacist's jacket, stood out among the old men. He counted the house as soon as he entered.

"There's only seven," he said, "with me."

Levinsky looked at his watch. "They're coming," he said. "I've got it in writing."

Just as Jack insisted that he had to leave before he lost his license, two men and a boy in his early teens marched up the stairs. The men's suits didn't fit, and the boy, who had a long thin neck, wore a white shirt that hung over his shoulders like an overcoat.

"The refugees," my father whispered to me. "I didn't know they were already in town."

Levinsky introduced them.

"Where are they from?" Mr. Dribben asked.

"From the camps," Levinsky said, "and from places that don't exist anymore."

We all shook hands with the newcomers. They spoke only Yiddish.

"Welcome to America," Mr. Dribben said to one of the men. "I can tell by your accent that you're from Galicia, right?"

The man didn't answer.

"Don't bother him with questions," Levinsky said in English. "They just got here this week. The Jewish agency is settling them in Grand Rapids. That's all you need to know."

"I asked a simple question," Dribben said, "and you jump on me."

"I told them," Levinsky said, "that in our shul they wouldn't have to talk until their stomachs hurt. They didn't want to come, but they're here to help us make the minyan. Let them daven and don't ask them where they're from and what kind of cholent their mother used to make."

Because of the refugees we were able to unwind the Torah scroll. Levinsky in his rich youthful voice sang the ancient words. Rocky watched for mistakes and called out corrections. I kept my eye on the refugees, especially the boy. He must be, I thought, what Rocky wanted me to be, a boy who studied Talmud at age four, who knew long sections by heart. I watched him, engrossed in prayers that I could read but not understand.

During a lull in the service, while Rocky and Levinsky scrolled through the Torah, looking for the remainder of that day's reading, my father spoke to the two men. I saw him nod his head. The boy stayed in his seat, his face concentrating on the prayer books.

"Until this week the men didn't even know each other," my father whispered to me. "They're from separate countries. The Jewish agency rented them a house; one family lives upstairs, the other downstairs."

At the table where the Torah lay spread open, blind Mr. Bookholder came up, touched the place where Levinsky was reading, and leaned down to kiss the scroll with his lips. Rocky and Levinsky, on either side of the Torah, were as happy as bridegrooms. Near the end of the reading, Levinsky motioned for the boy to step forward. He shook his head. I saw the panic in his eyes.

"It's okay," Rocky told him in Yiddish.

The boy stepped up to say the simple blessing. He didn't know any of the words. Rocky said each word, and the boy repeated after him. Even the worst students in our after-school Hebrew class knew the simple blessing. Five-year-olds knew it, and here was this guy with a big round face and a trace of a beard who had come from Europe and didn't know anything. I was surprised that Rocky didn't scold him or tell him to sit down.

I tried not to stare at him when he came back to his seat. His father shook his hand, and so did my father, who signaled me. I stood up and walked to him. I shook the boy's hand, too.

After the service ended everyone crossed the street to our house. Bashy and Gootie had set out cups for wine. They arranged plates of strudel and sponge cake. My father brought out a bottle of whiskey and made sure he poured the first drinks for the refugee men.

They spoke Yiddish, but in accents unfamiliar to me. Gootie, always hoping, asked them both if they had encountered her brother in the camps. The men shook their heads when Gootie showed them the photograph of her brother's family standing in front of their house, the boys with short haircuts like the young refugee.

Rocky led the boy who hadn't known the blessing over to me. "Talk to him," Rocky said.

We stood looking at one another.

"How old are you?" I asked in Yiddish.

"Fourteen," he told me; then he asked me where I was from.

"From here," I said, "from Grand Rapids."

"But they don't speak Yiddish in Grand Rapids," he said.

"In our house we do."

He asked if I knew English, too, and to prove it I spoke a few sentences. He told me he wanted to learn to speak like that right away. His name was Moshe. He said he had been in New York and then come directly to Grand Rapids.

"I haven't been to New York," I said. Then I asked him the question I had to ask. "How come you don't know Hebrew?" I asked. "Didn't you study in a yeshiva?"

"No," he said.

Bashy whisked him away to offer more cake and strudel, but I had some ammunition to use against Rocky the next time he told me that in Europe all the boys studied Talmud and knew a hundred times more than I did.

Levinsky reminded everyone that the following Saturday he needed each of them again. He didn't have to worry. On the third week there weren't enough chairs. The refugees were the draw.

People wanted to see them, to offer them hospitality and household items that they might need.

When we saw that there were more than ten men, my father and I went to the big synagogue, which seemed like an auditorium in comparison. The rabbi, when he spoke, announced that the ropes had been removed and people could now sit anywhere they chose. I could hardly wait to tell Rocky that he had won, but he learned in a more impressive way. Seymour Grossman, the president of the synagogue, came over to invite Rocky to return. "Everyone misses you," he said. "Sit where you want; make as much noise as you want; just come back."

"It's too late," Rocky told him. "I've got my own shul."

"You know there can't be two shuls," Seymour said. "There's barely enough people for one. Come back."

"Never," Rocky told him.

Seymour went across the street for a tour of the competition. Rocky liked him. Years ago he had been Max's friend.

"The refugees," Seymour said, "they really should come to the big shul. They need to meet people; they need help."

"They like our shul," Rocky said. "They don't need you and they don't need your rabbis."

"They're not religious," Seymour said. "They weren't before the war and they're not now, and they do need us and they need everything else."

We invited the refugees to eat with us on Friday night, but they already had invitations for a month in advance. Everyone noticed them as they walked down Eighth Street, where the Jewish Charities had rented them a two-story house with an upstairs porch that extended along one side of the upper floor. I walked past the house on my way to school and saw the boy sometimes on the porch, looking out at the street.

After a few weeks the refugees stopped coming. There was a minyan without them—even without Jack Remes, who put his foot down about abandoning the sick. When Levinsky went to investigate, he couldn't find the refugees. Both families had moved out. One of the neighbors told him that the two families didn't get along; someone else said they had moved to be closer to the school where the boy studied English. They had no telephone, and Levinsky wasn't even sure of their last names.

Without them my father and I decided to go to Rocky's shul in case the necessary ten didn't show up. We were there when the real surprise happened. Both Rocky and Levinsky looked at the door regularly, hoping for the refugees. When the newcomer walked in Rocky saw him first.

"Get out," Rocky yelled.

I recognized the man. A few months earlier I had seen him in front of the Majestic Theater, where he was handing out pamphlets. He was younger than Rocky and Levinsky but in his mid-sixties, at least. A tall, thin man, he looked Jewish even without the yarmulke he wore to identify himself.

He had not been smiling as he offered his free literature to people as they left the theater. Because I knew who he was, I watched with fascination, but almost everyone else ignored him. As soon as the crowd exited he walked away. He hadn't offered me a booklet, but I saw the cross on the outer page. I ran home to tell Gootie what I had seen.

"The poor soul," Gootie said. "Look what can happen to a person."

We called him the *mishumed,* the apostate. His daughter was married to a clothing store owner and came to the synagogue on the High Holy Days. There was nothing unusual about her, and her father, until he walked into the Mel Trotter Mission on Monroe Avenue, had been like the other immigrants, a workingman who sacrificed for his children.

Because he wasn't an important man in the Jewish community, his conversion didn't cause a stir. People were upset only when they saw him in public, as I had, distributing Christian literature.

"If he wanted to be a goy," Gootie said, "he should have gone somewhere else so he wouldn't shame his family." But she refused to believe that he had actually become a Christian. She blamed, as usual, the evil eye. Someone had cursed him; it wasn't his fault.

"He didn't do it for any reason. An old man doesn't just go crazy and become a missionary."

Rocky had no interest in explanations. Half a foot shorter and more than ten years older than the apostate, he took off his tallis and prepared to throw the *mishumed* out of the shul. Several of the men restrained him. The *mishumed* said nothing until Levinsky, much calmer than Rocky, walked over to speak to him. Levinsky didn't shake his hand, but he didn't threaten him, either.

"If he stays," Rocky said, "I'm leaving."

The *mishumed* conferred with Levinsky and then walked down the stairs.

"If you want to pray," Rocky yelled to him, "go to church."

There was no minyan, but the appearance of the *mishumed* overshadowed the failure to reach ten.

During the week all we talked about was the *mishumed*. Everyone had an opinion. Gootie thought that the evil eye must have been lifted as mysteriously as it had appeared. Rocky wouldn't budge. The man was an outcast. People from the big shul telephoned with questions. Nobody was entirely certain whether the man was a Jew or a Christian.

"He says he's a Christian; he stands downtown and tells people about Jesus. How can you say he's a Jew?" Rocky said.

Gootie argued from history. "He's circumcised, he had a Jewish mother, and for more than sixty years he was a Jew—a few pieces of paper that he gives to strangers don't change anything."

"We didn't start a shul," Rocky said, "to make a place for the *mishumed*."

Levinsky, the president, made the ruling decision. "He's a Jew," he said, "but after what he's done, he's not like other Jews."

They decided to treat the *mishumed* the way a suicide is treated at the cemetery—buried away from the rest of the community. Levinsky set up a wooden screen. If the *mishumed* came, he could sit by himself. Levinsky also argued for common civility.

"If a gentile would walk in," he asked Rocky, "would you throw him out?"

"Of course not," Rocky said, "unless it was the drunkard from downstairs."

"Then even if he's a gentile, let him stay. We won't count him for the minyan; he's a guest, a visitor. If he wants to pray, he can pray. That's his business."

The *mishumed* didn't return, and when the excitement died down neither did the curious. The blind man died. The colder weather kept the less committed old men home. Rocky and Levinsky, after a few months, were the only regulars at their synagogue. They stood beside the Torah as they prayed, but without a minyan they couldn't read from it. One Saturday Levinsky had a cold and only Rocky came to their synagogue.

When Gootie called her brother Leo, he didn't object. Leo and Yachey arrived one day to take charge of their investment.

Yachey refused even to walk into the old house. "You call this a shul?" she said. "No wonder nobody came." Leo drove the Torah to Mt. Pleasant, where some Dow Chemical workers had joined with the local shop owners to start a synagogue. Gootie checked the cover to make sure her son's name would be secure in Mt. Pleasant.

Rocky didn't argue. "I'm glad to get the Torah out of there before someone steals it," he said. "Let it go where people can use it."

When all traces of prayer had been removed, Gootie put out a FOR RENT sign. I worried that Rocky would leave again, but what happened at the bakery kept him close to home.

Chapter 17

*N*ate Wolf, a big man in a double-breasted suit, sat at our dining room table. Gootie brought out the glass carafe and two shot glasses.

"Rocky," Nate said, "I've heard about you from everybody. When I tell people I might buy the American Bakery, all I hear is 'Rocky,' 'Rocky,' 'Rocky.' You must be some baker."

"The son of a bitches from the union won't let me work," Rocky said.

Nate swallowed his Seagram's and smacked his lips. He took a bite of the coffee cake that Gootie had put out. He chewed carefully without worrying about the crumbs that fell on his suit.

"Did you bake this?" Nate asked.

"My wife did," Rocky said. "I don't bake anything one at a time."

Nate finished a big slice, then had a second shot of Seagram's. Rocky waited on the edge of his seat.

"If you'd baked this," Nate said, "I'd be asking myself—'Is

this the man I need?' I'm going to run a bakery. I'm going to need bakers."

"You want me," Rocky said, "I'll start right now."

"I didn't even buy the place yet," Nate said. "I came down to look things over. If I do buy, I'll expand. This won't be a little shop waiting for the weekends anymore—we'll give the big boys a run for the money.

"You know what people want?" Nate asked. "Pumpernickel. In New York there are bakeries that make a fortune only on pumpernickel—rolls, bagels, kaisers, everything pumpernickel."

Rocky made a face. "It's too heavy for a roll."

"Not in New York," Nate Wolf said. "In New York people know how to eat pumpernickel. If I buy, I'm getting out of birthday cakes, out of cookies."

"Good," Rocky said, "get rid of the doughnuts, too."

"We'll see," Nate Wolf said. He asked Rocky about the other bakers, the supplies, and the big customers.

"I've been retired ten years," Rocky said. "Ask Philip."

"How much of the business is Jewish?" Nate asked.

"On Friday," Rocky said, "we have challah. Nobody else does. Everybody buys their challah from us."

"What does that amount to? Fifty loaves, maybe? A hundred?"

"Less," Rocky said, "but wait until you taste my challah."

Nate came into the kitchen to meet Gootie. He looked over our yard and the neighborhood. He spoke a reasonable Yiddish.

We all went outside to see the yellow Studebaker that he drove all the way from New York.

"I'm not the kind of a man who does anything halfway," Nate Wolf said. "If I decide to buy the American Bakery, then that's exactly what I'll do. To me it isn't money. I'm not worried about making money. A baker always makes money—right, Rocky?"

Rocky nodded. "People always need bread."

"That's right," Nate said, "pumpernickel."

Gootie started asking Rocky at every meal if he wanted pumpernickel.

"You laugh," he said. "Shoemaker's daughter, what do you know. Nate Wolf is a real baker. He'll give this town what it needs."

To Rocky, Nate entered the American Hall of Fame alongside Abe Lincoln and Babe Ruth. He got in easily—no questions asked. All Nate said was, "Screw the union. If I take over the bakery, nobody's gonna tell me Rocky can't work."

We waited to see what would happen. Philip had no other offers for the bakery. Nate was serious. He wanted to buy, but he had no money. Philip, urged by his daughters to retire, took a small down payment.

Nate Wolf called Rocky when he returned to Grand Rapids. "Give me a few days," he said. "Then I will personally see that you have a job."

The New Yorker kept his word. In the Studebaker he picked Rocky up for his first Saturday night at the American Bakery. Rocky, who always waited for the Sabbath to arrive, this time couldn't wait for it to end. At twilight he started looking at the sky for three stars.

"You're too old to work all night," Gootie said. "Go a few hours in the morning or the afternoon. Your babies won't starve if you work less."

"Nate needs me," Rocky said. "A night is nothing to me. I can work all night and all the next day, too."

He did. At seven A.M. on Sunday, after he had already worked twelve hours, he refused to leave.

"He's my kind of baker," Nate said when he came to work at about ten and gave Rocky a ride home.

Saturday night became Rocky's regular job. For all his talk Nate didn't buck the union. He risked letting Rocky work only on Saturday night and he paid him in cash, but to Rocky the money didn't matter. He was back in the place he loved. Every Sunday morning I went to the American Bakery to persuade Rocky to leave.

I wanted the task for reasons of my own. The American Bakery, on Bridge Street, the main thoroughfare of the west side, was only a few blocks from the Town Theatre, which showed triple features every Sunday. I would coax Rocky out of the bakery in stages, the way he woke me in the mornings. My deadline was noon, when the Town began the Sunday program with a Flash Gordon serial. I would get to the bakery about eleven, let Rocky know I was there, then enjoy a leisurely doughnut in the salesroom. On Sunday most of the business was Polish ladies on their way home from church. They bought more sweets than bread.

Depending on when the sun had set Saturday night, Rocky had sometimes been working fifteen hours by the time I walked into the working area to fetch him.

I would begin by reminding him that he was supposed to work only an eight-hour shift.

"His grandma tells him to say that," Rocky would tell Joe Post, his fellow cake man. "To her a minute after eight hours is overtime. The bread doesn't look at a clock; it's ready when it's ready."

"He sleeps standing up," Joe Post told me. "No kidding, he stands by the table and closes his eyes for ten or fifteen minutes, and he does that every few hours. That's how he can keep going. Rocky's like a horse."

"You sleep all the time," Rocky said. "That's why I've got to work twice as hard."

"You're okay, Rocky," Joe Post said, "as long as you're not the boss. If you were ever in charge, you'd work us to death."

"If Philip had worked you a little more, he wouldn't have had to sell the bakery," Rocky said.

Joe was too big around the waist to keep his trousers up with a belt. You could see his suspenders on either side of the apron, discolored by ancient specks of flour.

For my second attempt at luring Rocky from the bakery I would reenter the back room and watch him work. I asked only one question: "How long?"

"When I'm finished, I'll be finished. Go home."

I wouldn't leave. After five or ten minutes he would take hold of my shoulder and lead me to the door.

"Tell the shoemaker's daughter to leave me alone. I've gotta work."

By my third entry, Joe Post would be laughing too much to work.

"You're still here," Rocky would yell. "You could have been home by now."

I would then announce the hours he had worked: twelve, fourteen, fifteen, sixteen, whatever the number. "I'm going to tell the union," I said.

He knew I wouldn't, but it was the signal that I meant business. If his hands were working the dough, he would stop and pass the heavy yellow clump to Joe Post—then our bargaining began in earnest.

"A half hour, until the bread comes out of the oven."

I would check my watch, and Joe would call me a "foreman." I gave Rocky until 11:55; then he would pull off his apron, wash his hands, and hurry down Bridge Street with me to the Town. As soon as he sat down he fell asleep. He slept through Flash Gordon, the Movietone News, and the cartoon. Long before the triple feature began he would be snoring.

In most theaters an usher would have come over to ask us to leave, but the Town on all days, especially on Sunday, was as noisy as a playground. We cheered for Flash; we even cheered for whoever seemed like the good guys in the news.

During quiet minutes Rocky's snoring caused some laughs, but we were all regulars. After a few weeks the kids knew who Rocky was just as I knew who the Polish women in babushkas were in the bakery salesroom. Between the snoring and the cheering I watched Abbot and Costello, Ma and Pa Kettle, the Cisco Kid, and Hopalong Cassidy.

After his long shift Rocky would usually sleep through a double feature and wake up as if he were startled during the third movie.

"Let's go," he said. "It's too noisy here to rest."

I didn't argue, even if I wanted to know how the movie ended. In the bakery, filled with adrenaline and the exaltation of being back at work, he seemed as if he could have worked another twenty-four hours if I hadn't arrived to pull him away. But after his movie nap, he was a tired man. He walked slowly on our way home, ate something, and then went right to sleep.

Gootie didn't taunt him about working so long. She just put out his food. He would sleep straight through from four or five in the afternoon until the next morning.

I liked those Sundays at the bakery and then the Town Theatre and would have gladly continued until I outgrew the triple features. But Nate Wolf had other plans. He expanded the American Bakery. Pumpernickel even showed up in a few supermarkets.

"He's a good businessman," Rocky said, "and he knows how to make a dough, but he's not in the bakery enough. He's out selling."

Gootie didn't like Nate. He was a bachelor but had no interest in any of the local unmarried women. People said he had a girlfriend in New York and a new one closer by in Grand Haven. She had been seen in the bakery, a big Dutch woman who walked behind the counter to use the phone whenever she wanted to and told everyone she was Nate's friend.

"He'll sell out as soon as he can," Gootie said. "If you come to live someplace, you don't run away from getting married."

"Leave the man alone," Rocky said. "He's thinking about his business, not women."

"That shows what you know," Gootie said. "If Mr. Pumpernickel told you it was a workday, you'd run on Friday night, too, anything to make Mr. Pumpernickel happy. How did you live so many years without him?"

Gootie told me she had nothing against Nate Wolf, but she thought he was too much of a big shot to own a bakery.

"He's a boss," she said. "Philip worked alongside the men, but this Mr. Pumpernickel spends his nights in Grand Haven. He's got his real bakery there. You'll see—one of these days he'll leave in a minute."

She was almost right. Nate didn't leave, but he made a mistake.

"It's nothing," he said when Rocky confronted him. "A wrong delivery, that's all. Next week I'll send it back."

Rocky had found three drums of lard in the storeroom. Lard would make everything in the bakery unkosher.

"I'll give you a mistake," Rocky said. He went for Nate Wolf's cheeks with his fists.

Joe Post held Rocky in the air until the owner could escape. "We didn't use it," Joe Post said. "Nothing happened, Rocky. Take it easy."

Before he told any of us, Rocky walked up Michigan Hill to the rabbi's office. He hadn't talked to the young rabbi in more than two years.

"I found lard," he said.

In the rabbi's car they drove to the bakery.

Joe Post had rolled the steel cans of shortening to the rear of the storeroom. "We never used it," he told the rabbi. "The driver left it by mistake. Rocky just went nuts when he saw it."

Nate Wolf told the rabbi the same story. "A little mistake," he said, "but no lard ever got into bread. How could it when Rocky works here?"

Rocky wanted Philip to reclaim ownership.

"In the contract it doesn't say he has to keep the bakery kosher," Philip said, "but I never thought he'd change it, not without telling people."

A yellowing certificate hung near the outer door of the bakery. After checking the storeroom, the rabbi took down the certificate stating that the products were kosher.

Nate watched. He remained calm. "It won't make a bit of difference," he said. "Nobody cares except the old man. The bread will be as good as ever."

To anyone who wanted to question him, Nate stated his innocence and showed his storeroom filled with vegetable shortening, but for Rocky and Levinsky and a few others, the American Bakery had changed forever. No one in our family ever went in again.

You couldn't mention pumpernickel to Rocky, and we stopped going to the Town Theatre on Sundays. Whatever we didn't bake in our kitchen we now had to order frozen from Detroit. The bread came every two weeks with the meat and chickens.

Nate Wolf gave kosher one more try. He offered to allow inspection of his ingredients, but the rabbi turned him down. He said the bakery could no longer be trusted.

This rabbinic decision made Rocky change his mind. He hadn't gone to the synagogue since the rabbi had tried to force him into being a more orderly congregant. By taking a stand against Nate Wolf, the young man proved himself.

When, on Saturday morning, the rabbi announced that the American Bakery was no longer kosher, Rocky was present in his usual seat in the back row. The rabbi didn't ask him to move, and when the rabbi spoke Rocky didn't interrupt.

Saturday afternoon Levinsky scoffed, "All you wanted was a chance to go back. You were just waiting. Not me—I'm never going back."

But when Rocky told his friend that the portrait of the founder had moved back to the main lobby, Levinsky decided to have a look. The next week he was at the synagogue, too. He liked what he saw—himself in 1917 as handsome as he said he was.

With Levinsky in his seat at one end of the room and Rocky mumbling from the other corner, the synagogue regained its proportion.

Nate Wolf didn't suffer, either. He built a restaurant and a pizza parlor, and his pumpernickel became famous throughout the city.

PART II

Chapter 18

*T*he places that Gootie had united for me, Grand Rapids and Serei, came unraveled. One document did it—a driver's license. When I started to leave our house in the evenings, Gootie considered the examples of male roaming that she knew, her husband and her brothers. "They went to America," she said. "Where are you going?"

I didn't know it at the time, but that was my destination, too. To get there I didn't have to cross the ocean, merely the Grand River. On the east side of the river everyone spoke English, and the categories "Jew" and "goy" didn't even seem to matter. The only passport anyone needed was a car.

My journey to America happened so fast that both Gootie and I were dazed by it. One day I was still her little Mottele, drinking Sanka coffee in the kitchen as I listened to the stories about Serei and helped her plan for the next big event, a Jewish holiday or a trip to Muskegon or Alma. The next day I became a teenager.

Neither of us understood what was happening. I thought I was bored at home. Gootie suspected worse.

"Do you go to meetings in basements?" she asked me.

It was the era of basement "rec" rooms. The suburbs went underground. In the new homes people built basement rooms especially for their children. I admitted that I went to basements, but not to meetings.

"Do they have speakers who tell you to take over the schools and the factories?"

"They play records," I said. "People dance. Sometimes there's a pool table."

"Don't go," she warned me. "They'll tell you it's a party. Then all of a sudden they bring out a picture of Lenin and you'll be marching down the street in a parade until the police run after you. From here there's no place to run to. You're already in America."

To calm her fears I told her the truth. "I don't go anywhere most of the time," I admitted. "I just drive around."

"You don't stop?"

"I stop for red lights."

"You don't talk to people? You don't go into someone's house and drink ginger ale and say hello to their parents?"

"No," I said, "not unless there's a party, and then—"

"I know," she said. "You go to the basements."

"At least in the car I have privacy," I told her.

"What's privacy?"

"To be alone," I said.

"God forbid," she said. "Nobody should be alone."

"That's what I want. I'm the only person I know who shares a bedroom with his grampa."

"All right," she suggested, "the girls are at college. You want to be alone? Take over their room—two beds, two dressers, a radio—they've got everything. Who else has such luxuries?"

"Everyone," I told her, but I took her up on the offer. I did move into my sisters' room. I told Rocky as casually as I could that I would be moving downstairs. "When the girls come back for vacation, I'll be back," I said.

"You don't go to sleep until midnight anyway," he said. "Pretty soon you'll be sleeping in the car, too. Do what you want."

I waited until Rocky was out of the house before I carried my pillow and blankets downstairs. Gootie came in to make sure I was comfortable. She declared the problem of my roaming solved. "You want to be alone—here you're alone. When you close both doors, not even the cat can get in."

After supper when I asked my father for the car keys Gootie looked surprised. "Where are you going? You've got the girls' room. Why do you have to leave?"

"I'm not going to stay there all the time. I'll still go out."

"Out," she said, "all you say now is 'out.' Everything a person could want is in the house—a telephone, a television, every kind of food. What else can a person want?"

I was already starting the car when I saw Gootie waving to me. She hurried as fast as she could. The Persian lamb coat that Yachey gave her wasn't even buttoned.

"I'm coming," she said, "to see what you do."

If Rocky had said that, I wouldn't have been surprised; he liked to go places. Unless it was to visit one of her brothers, Gootie hardly left the house. The kitchen had everything she needed. A miraculous self-defrosting refrigerator, a sink with more hot water than anyone could use, a row of ten Sanka coffee cans filled with lentils, split peas, barley, egg noodles, and, her favorite, Minute rice—enough dried food to feed us for weeks if locusts arrived or our money became worthless or gangs of hoodlums descended to make life harder for Jews. She had all the necessities at hand and the luxuries as well. At night, before she went to bed, Gootie wiped clean with a sponge her prize possessions, three stoves.

The Tappan gas range was merely utilitarian. Everyone had a gas stove—it was cheaper than electricity and cooked faster. But on Friday night, when Jewish law forbids lighting the oven, gas presented a problem. Gootie worried that lighting the oven be-

fore the Sabbath began and leaving it on all night would asphyx-
iate us. If we had a wood-burning stove in the middle of the room,
as her family had in Serei, there would be no problem: if the fire
went out, you were merely cold, not poisoned by invisible fumes.

She refused to allow the gas stove to remain on all night. This
meant that we would have to eat cold food on the Sabbath, no
way to celebrate the day in which God himself rested. She solved
the problem by buying a second stove, a Kelvinator electric—
topped with four burners. We used the electric oven only for
keeping Sabbath food warm. All night chicken and prune and
potato *tsimmes* sat in round aluminum pots. Dry as beef jerky, but
steaming hot, our Sabbath meals never endangered us.

The second stove made her feel wealthy. "Who else has two
stoves?" she asked when she needed reassurance. The third stove,
the one that put us over the top, she couldn't resist. I showed her
the picture in the newspaper. We went to the electric company
office, where a woman in an apron demonstrated right in the
middle of the big room where people were paying bills and apply-
ing for new service. I filled out the forms—Gootie marked her X
on the dotted line. We paid our bills on time; the credit would be
no problem. For ten dollars a month we bought a built-in rotisserie oven with a rotating spit. If we had wanted to, we could
have had a luau for the Sabbath, roasted chickens, or shish
kebab—we even had the pointed sticks included with the oven.
The rotisserie oven had a clock that worked and an automatic
timer. We could have put in raw meat and returned hours later to
find it browned on all sides with gravy ready in the remarkable
bottom tray.

Every once in a while Gootie would turn on the oven's interior light, push the rotisserie switch, and watch through the
smoky window as the stainless-steel arm rotated slowly, heating
only her pleasure at having lived to possess a third oven. We
never used it.

We had Melmac dishes that we didn't use, either, but Gootie
and I took them out of the cupboard from time to time so that we
could drop them on the linoleum floor and watch them not

break. We had thirty-six steak knives with plastic "bone" grips that I found advertised in a magazine at the close-out price of six for a dollar. We had two sets of stainless-steel silverware that we got completely free by cutting the word "Sunkist" from orange skins and sending the shriveled words by the hundreds to Sunkist in return for the silverware.

For the kitchen nothing was too good. Gootie approved of everything that came in white enamel. She had never gone to the drugstore, to the IGA, not even to the Widdicombe parking lot to watch me play baseball. The three stoves were her continents. Suddenly, to understand my roaming, she followed me to the car to learn about what I did when I left the house after dark.

She sat in the backseat. Usually I stopped to pick up a friend, but with her in the backseat I was conscious that I had no destination. I pointed out the landmarks—the library, the hotel. She knew what they were. After two circuits I asked her if she was ready to go home.

"This is it," I said, "you've seen—that's all there is."

"You go around in circles," she said.

I couldn't deny it.

"Like a dog. For this you don't need a car."

"Everyone has a car," I told her.

"If it's so important to use a car," she said, "take me somewhere."

We stopped at Kewpies, a drive-in restaurant. She had never seen outdoor speakers. I ordered Sanka coffee for Gootie, and when a waitress put the cup on a tray that hooked over the window, I finally had evidence of the value of a car.

"You don't have to go inside; they bring everything right to you," I said.

"I'd rather go inside," she said. "It's too cold." I sent our order back and tipped the waitress.

Nobody over twenty-five would go to Kewpies unless they were forced. Gootie walked slowly, taking it all in. Kewpie dolls were the motif—cherubs decorated the door handles and the menu. Ceramic cupids hung from the wall, their arrows pointed at whoever entered.

Tortured love blared from the jukebox. Teenagers ate pre-McDonald's hamburgers as they rested, temporarily, from driving the circuit.

I didn't see anybody I knew. I tried to hurry Gootie to a booth and positioned myself with my back to the door. Gootie kept her Persian lamb coat on. Even though I couldn't see the room, I knew that everyone was looking at us.

When the waitress arrived, Gootie shook her head. I ordered coffee for her and orange juice for me.

"You have to order," I whispered to her. "They won't let you sit here if you don't buy something."

"What else do they sell?" she asked.

"Just food," I said. "It's a restaurant. You'll drink your coffee and then we'll go."

She watched the more socially confident boys who dared to walk up to a booth full of girls. She watched the parade to the bathrooms and the small crowd at the jukebox. Even if there had been room, nobody would have danced. People came to Kewpies to look at one another. The boys wore their trousers low around their hips and grew Elvis sideburns. The girls wore saddle shoes and tight sweaters. Even in the restaurant people kept moving—to the jukebox, to another booth, to check the parking lot. Temporarily without our cars, we treated each booth like a car without windows. We could hear better and we were saving on gas, but we kept traveling. Gootie had never seen such aimlessness. Watching her watch teenagers made me feel much less like one.

I had been to Kewpies a hundred times, but this time I saw it through her eyes. She didn't have to say anything to make me wonder why I was looking at girls I didn't dare to speak to and would never see again, why I was overpaying for coffee and orange juice when I wasn't even thirsty. I felt ashamed that Gootie saw me as I was, as I had become—a sixteen-year-old more connected to a car than to my ancestors.

A boy who knew me came over to say hello. I nodded. I didn't introduce him to Gootie, and I was grateful that he left immediately, even though there was space in our small booth. I drank my juice in two swallows. Gootie sipped her coffee.

"Who owns the restaurant?" she asked.

"I don't know," I said, "and I don't care."

"The owner must be here," she said. She looked around the crowded restaurant but saw only teenagers. "He does a good business."

I knew what was coming.

"I'm not interested," I said. "Don't tell me to think about opening a restaurant or opening a store. Just drink your coffee and let's get out of here."

"Don't be in such a hurry," she said. "Driving around in circles can wait. Here there are people—they're talking to one another; they're doing business . . ."

"They're teenagers," I reminded her. "They're not doing business."

"It won't hurt you," she said, "to talk to someone. You don't have to sit alone."

"I'm not alone. I'm with you," I said.

"I like to hear people talk," she said. "Call someone over . . . not her . . ." She pointed to the waitress. "She only wants money."

"I'm not calling anyone over, and if you say 'mister' and motion to somebody, I'm going to stand up and leave and you'll have to get home yourself."

When we got home Rocky was waiting up for both of us. I saw his hands cupped around his eyes as he looked out the window. He was more angry at Gootie than at me.

"It's not enough that he's running around," Rocky said. "You're starting, too."

"Go to sleep," Gootie said, "and dream about being the tenth man at a minyan."

He looked at his watch. The gold-colored Speidel band

seemed out of place as he stood in his long underwear. "Are you coming upstairs or not?" he asked me.

"I told you, I moved to the girls' room." He still waited for me. "For privacy," I added. "I'm sixteen. I don't want to share a room with my grandpa." I gave Gootie a look that was my version of Rocky glaring. "And I don't want to take you to Kewpies. I want to be like everyone else."

"You think you're the first person who had grandparents?" Gootie said. "Everyone had them except Adam and Eve."

"Sleep wherever you want," Rocky said, "and you can wake yourself up in the morning, too."

"I will," I said. He stormed upstairs. Gootie took off her fur coat and went to her spot at the kitchen table.

"Now we can drink coffee," she said, "without paying for it."

"I've had enough coffee," I said. "I'm going to sleep. And from now on everything is going to be different."

Gootie propped her stiff leg on a chair, then blew her nose. "Are you still going to eat and sleep?" she asked.

"You know what I mean," I said. "I'm not going to explain anymore." I went to my new room.

The girls had the biggest room in the house, furnished in what my mother thought was the most modern style. The rest of us had metal-frame beds; the girls had mahogany French provincial twin beds and matching dressers. They had wool blankets instead of featherbeds.

I turned on the radio and the light beside the bed. I had an entire empty bed to toss my clothes on. I reveled in my sudden privacy—no Rocky snoring, no tenants in the apartment behind, arguing with one another. I could stay up as late as I wanted reading. I could do everything in that room but sleep. I missed Rocky's snoring. By about three A.M. I had as much privacy as I could stand. I went back to the room I shared with Rocky. In the morning he woke me at seven.

"Thank God," Gootie said when she saw that I had returned. "Thank God that you don't want to be alone anymore." But she understood that where I slept wasn't the real problem. She called in her expert adviser, her brother Joe.

Her brother Leo was too rich to be involved in family problems, but Joe, like Gootie, still worked in a Serei frame of reference. "Don't worry," Joe said to me before the three of us had our conference, "I'll explain everything to her."

Gootie served Joe a full meal as soon as he sat down. Because he was a widower, she knew he was always hungry. I drank a Coke and laughed to myself as I listened to Gootie's description of the drive-in restaurant.

Joe nodded his head. He tucked his napkin over his tie. He always wore a suit and a tie and a hat, and he was on the lookout for a new outfit. He needed thirty-eight short-portly just to fit his waist. I had been to a half dozen stores with him without finding his size. Gootie considered Joe a man of the world, a businessman; everyone else thought of him as what he was, a retired farmer.

"I've seen those places," Joe said. "We've got them in Muskegon, too. They charge a quarter for a cup of coffee. They call them 'red-light houses.'"

Gootie covered her eyes with her hands. "He'll get diseases," she said. "He'll lose his mind. Maybe it's already happening."

"Don't worry about that," Joe said. "They're clean. Nurses inspect them, and the police keep watch over the whole thing. They had these places in Russia, too. All the soldiers went."

"It's a restaurant," I said. "That's all."

"He's telling you the truth," Joe said. "They have food and beer, not just women. They're in bad neighborhoods, but they can charge high rent anyway."

"He's a child," Gootie said. "He barely knows the difference between a man and a woman."

Joe winked at me. "He knows."

When he finished his meal he made me an offer.

"It's a golden opportunity," Gootie said. "Joe himself will teach you business."

"What business?" I asked Joe.

"Collecting rent," he said.

"How hard is that?"

"Harder than you think," he said. "Not everyone wants to pay, and sometimes they want to and they don't have any money."

"You'll like it," Gootie said. "You'll drive around all day with Joe. He'll let you drive his car—you won't even need to buy one."

"It doesn't sound like much of a job," I said. "What do you do? Ring the doorbell and ask for money?"

"You don't have to ask," Joe said. "They all know me. They like me. The kids yell, 'It's him.' You go in, they offer you coffee, you sit down . . ."

"You see," Gootie said, "you're already learning."

"Anybody can do that," I said. "What's the job?"

"The job is to walk out with money and to leave the tenant a receipt."

"That's business," Gootie said, "and then you drive to the bank and put the money in and the bank gives you a receipt."

"That's not a job I want," I said.

"He'd rather drive around all night without collecting a penny," Gootie said. "What's the difference? Driving is driving. This way you can go with Joe and he'll pay you, too."

"And whenever you want to," Joe said, "you can spend the night in Muskegon at my place."

My goal at that time was to earn enough money to buy a used car. All the boys in my class wanted the same thing—a car was the key to independence. Joe offered to pay me a dollar an hour to drive around with him, so during spring vacation I decided to give collecting a try. I would spend the week with Joe.

"You'll come back a businessman," Gootie said.

Chapter 19

I took the Greyhound bus to Muskegon. Joe lived two blocks from the bus station in the downstairs apartment of an old house. He had a sectional couch that he had pushed together to make a bed for me. The back of the couch, the dining table, the two end tables, the Victrola, and even the refrigerator were covered with white crochet work made by his wife during her years of heart failure. All the pieces had turned yellow.

"Clean as a whistle," Joe said. "You're gonna like it here."

Only his safe had no crocheted covering. It was too big. He kept it in the middle of the living room, covered with a plastic tablecloth. Dark red flowers on the tablecloth disguised the combination knob. I had always played with the safe whenever we visited Joe, so it didn't seem like unusual furniture to me. He used to tell me that someday he'd let me open it.

"It's better than a bank," he said. "If I'd kept my money in here during the Depression, I'd be a rich man now."

We didn't go anywhere that first day. Joe showed me his collection of records. He still had the old seventy-eight of "Getzel at the Ball Game," about a dozen cantorial albums, and an album of early 1940s patriotic songs called *I'm Gonna Slap That Dirty Little Jap*.

In his refrigerator he had a quart bottle of milk, a month past its deadline. In the tiny freezer were four lamb chops and some aluminum pots filled with frozen chicken soup that Gootie prepared for him.

While he ate the lamb chops I went back to the bus station to buy potato chips and pretzels for my dinner.

At night I couldn't sleep. I felt the itchy material of the couch right through the sheet, and the sections kept moving apart every time I turned. Joe kept his teeth in a glass on top of the safe, and I could see them even when I closed my eyes. The safe bothered me, too. Gootie always worried that someone would break in to rob Joe. All his tenants knew he had a floor safe; so did anyone who walked past his house and looked through his thin curtains.

"Someone will come in and cut your throat," Gootie often warned her brother.

"If they do," he said, "they'll never open the safe."

I drank instant coffee at five; Joe was ready to go by six.

"We can't go yet," he said. "They don't like it when you wake them up, but if you don't get there early, they go to work and then to a tavern and you can forget about collecting."

I followed Joe's directions to Muskegon Heights. He didn't know the names of any streets; he navigated by landmarks—a church, a gas station, a big green house. I kept missing the landmarks. Finally I had to let him drive. I recognized the house in Muskegon Heights. It was the house he and Sarah and Louie had lived in.

"I didn't know you still owned this one," I said.

"You never sell a house," Joe said. "You can always earn something from it and sell it for more later."

I went to the door with Joe. The house looked the way I remembered it, but it had no grass—a two-story with vinyl siding made to resemble gray brick.

Nobody came to the door.

"Let's go," I said.

"They're here," Joe said.

We waited until I couldn't stand it any longer.

"There's nobody home. Let's go," I said.

Joe shook his head. He held his receipt book and a fountain pen. I went to the car to wait. Joe's Ford had no radio. I opened the glove compartment hoping for something to read, and I found a box of condoms—Trojans in dark brown foil, exactly like the ones some of the boys in my class carried in their wallets.

When Joe talked about whorehouses I thought he had mixed up the English phrases "fast food" and "red light." Now I wasn't so sure. I closed the glove compartment and then opened it again to check whether I had really seen the Trojans. I read the small print, looking for a date. I thought these might be antique Trojans like the little tin Tums case Joe used even though I had only seen Tums wrapped in paper. On his dining room table Joe had pages of the *Muskegon Chronicle* that were four or five years old. He'd owned his safe since 1909. The Trojans were too modern for him.

I heard the screen door slam. A man in suspenders came to the door. Joe went in. A few minutes later he came out. Back in the car, he reached into his coat pocket and showed me cash.

"A hundred and sixty-five dollars," he said. "You see, you'd have missed it."

I wasn't thinking about the rent anymore.

"Clarence is always home," Joe said, "and he's always got the money, but he hates to pay. For Clarence you've got to wait."

I couldn't put Joe and the Trojans together. Gootie's brother, Serei, his potbelly, what he thought was stylish—wearing both a belt and suspenders—it didn't go with Trojans, the status item in high school. They were hard to get. You couldn't just walk into a store and buy them. You had to ask the pharmacist. At Remes Drug Store, the boys in school said, Jack wouldn't sell you Trojans unless you were married or at least engaged. I didn't even dare to mention Trojans at the drugstore. The word was loaded. It had connections to Marilyn Monroe and Jane Russell and Esther Williams, the hot names of that era. The word meant sex and beauty, not my great-uncle Joe.

He was happy with his collection. "You'll learn," he told me. "You've got to be patient. People don't want to let go of their money. They know they'll have to, but they like to wait until the last minute. I don't hold it against them. I'm like that myself."

"Joe," I told him, "I saw the Trojans in your glove compartment."

He didn't seem to know what I was talking about. I opened the glove compartment and held up the little box.

"Someone must have left that in the car," he said. "I give lots of people rides. If I'm going the same way, why should they take a bus?

"Now I'll show you something you'll really love," Joe said. He turned onto a dirt road, and after driving for a few minutes, he parked beside a plowed field.

"Where are we?" I asked.

"Section sixteen," he said.

I followed him out of the car.

"One hundred and sixty acres," Joe said. He raised his arm and arched to the right, demonstrating his great expanse to me. "Everyone wants to own land in section sixteen," he said.

"Why?" I asked.

"Onions," he said. "You can sell all your onions in Grant. They ship them all over the world from Grant. It's a big onion town. And we're not far from Ravenna. It's the best part of the country. Someday," he said, "part of this will belong to you. I told Gootie I would leave you the house in Muskegon Heights, too. She worries that you won't be able to make a living, but I told her that in America everyone makes a living. She's a smart woman, but she only knows women's things. That's why she wants me to teach you business."

The next day I told Joe that I would never be a good rent collector.

"I can see that," he said. "Maybe when you're older you'll try again." He drove me to the bus station.

That night I didn't go anywhere. I stayed home and sat in the kitchen with Gootie. I told her about Clarence, who didn't come to the door, and I emphasized how wise and patient her brother was. Gootie glowed.

"He was always smart," she said. "If he had stayed in Serei, he would have owned half the town."

I told her about the 160 acres of onions and about Joe's two-family house on Concord Avenue.

"You're on your way," she said, "but why did you come back so fast?"

"Joe told me I'm too young for collecting," I told her.

"Maybe so," she said, "but I'm glad you went. At least you've seen how to do it. Joe loves you. Who else does he have?"

I didn't tell Gootie that when Joe drove me to the bus station, I asked if I could have the box in the glove compartment.

"Take it," he said. He gave me ten dollars, too, my fee as a collector, but the Trojans were worth far more. What the other boys stole or were given by their big brothers came to me from an older source.

On the side of the crimped aluminum, right next to the name of the rubber company, it said "Made in USA." No doubt it was, but mine took the long route, by way of Serei.

Chapter 20

*E*ven though I didn't have my own car and lived only two blocks from school, parking became my biggest problem. A wealthy suburban district emptied its junior high into Union. The upper-middle-class sixteen-year-olds drove to school, and they looked for parking places. Rocky stood in front of the house and ordered them away. I didn't want the new students to know that he was my grandfather.

"They've got a right to park here," I told Rocky. "There are no signs; it's not a no-parking zone."

"They've got a right to park," Rocky said, "and I've got a right to tell 'em I don't want them here."

"They don't bother you; they park and then they go to school all day."

"That's what you think," Rocky said. "They don't stay all day. They leave early—one or two o'clock."

"Maybe they've got jobs."

He looked at me. "They're good-for-nothings. They don't

work. They sit in their cars at lunchtime and smoke. They bring girls into the cars. And the girls bring boys in."

He sat outside on balmy days, reading the Talmud, getting up every once in a while to yell at Larry across the street. On cold days he watched from indoors, then hurried out before the parallel parkers could finish their job.

"They drive their cars so fast around the block that their tires squeal," Rocky said. "They're liable to kill somebody." To stop them he stood on the corner and raised his fist at the drag racers.

By sixteen a lot of my old friends, the ones who knew Gootie and Rocky, had quit school for full-time jobs in gas stations or at the Fisher Body Plant. The new suburban students were different. They were the children of professional parents. They didn't take the shop courses that had been required for the rest of us. And Rocky was right: they didn't work, but they all had cars. Girls, in groups of twos and threes, watched the circling cars before deciding which one they'd choose for a ride. They picked their boyfriends based on horsepower and cubic inches. I barely knew this crowd. They avoided the shop majors, but in chemistry class random luck gave me the best-looking girl in the school as a lab partner. I couldn't look straight at her without staring. Sometimes she asked me to tie the black rubber apron around her neck. She copied my lab notebook because she didn't have time to do homework—after school she rode horses. One morning as I was about to leave for school, I saw Rocky ordering her away from our house.

After that, I had to change my schedule. I no longer left for school until everyone had parked. On most days I arrived a few minutes late. I could offer no excuse and had to endure warnings from Miss Pershbacher, the assistant principal, that I would not be admitted to any college, that I would be unemployable, that the tardiness would never be erased from my record.

I took the risk—and to avoid embarrassment at midday, I began to carry my lunch to school. This upset Gootie. Usually she had her breakfast as I ate lunch. We sat together, and she made certain that I had soup every day.

"I have to go to meetings," I told her.

"Why at lunchtime? You're in school all day," she said. "You have only an hour for lunch. Why do they have to make the meetings exactly when it's time to eat?"

I missed her as I sat in the study hall and ate alone, but I couldn't risk being seen at noon when all the suburbanites were cruising and Rocky was on patrol against them.

I overheard someone imitating his accent almost every day. For a few of the suburban boys it became a game to rile the old man. They drove by and started to back up in front of our driveway; then, as soon as he came after them, they burned rubber, drove around the block, and came back a few minutes later.

Gootie didn't mind because it gave him something to do. With me gone a lot of evenings and my sisters away at the University of Michigan, she lost her main sources of new material. There were not as many phone conversations to overhear, and she missed the lively arguments of the debate conferences my sisters used to host in our living room. She missed their yearly practices of the "I Speak for Democracy" contest. In order to laugh at America she needed more information. I reported less than my sisters had about school life. The more Gootie asked, the less I told.

She slept through Rocky's morning encounters with the parkers, but sometimes at noon she walked to the sunroom to see her husband in action. I told her to stay inside. I didn't want to see the suburban kids imitating her dragging her leg behind Rocky.

I was embarrassed by both of them and by the sudden sprouting of acne. With the acne Gootie tried to help. Eserkey, she told me, had pimples like mine in Odessa. "I was already going to doctors for my leg," she told me, "so once he went with me and we asked the biggest doctor in Odessa, the one who told me I needed mud from the Black Sea, what to do about the pimples. He looked at Eserkey—they don't have doctors like him in America—all he had to do was look. 'This boy needs to eat yeast,' he said. 'That will cure him.'"

Every day when she took her high-blood-pressure pill, she

mixed my yeast potion in orange juice. When it didn't help she suggested that I put the yeast directly on my face. That didn't help, either, but Gootie proclaimed me cured. "All you have to do is wait," she said. "By the time Eserkey got married his face was like snow."

With my skin in bloom and Rocky on patrol, the girl I thought about all the time appeared. I was outside with Rocky, safe, I thought, because it was almost dark and school had been dismissed hours earlier. She saw me and pulled up in front of the house.

"I forgot my stuff," she said, "so I came back, but nobody's there. The school's all locked up. Can I borrow your chemistry book?"

I wanted to say I didn't live there, but Rocky, who hadn't paid attention to what she said, asked her who she was.

"We're lab partners," she said. She pulled her car closer to the curb.

"I didn't know you lived so close to school," she said. "God, you're lucky. You can sleep until eight."

I didn't want to invite her into the house, where Gootie might try to interview her in pidgin English, but if I left her at the curb, I knew Rocky would make her move her car. She had a '57 Chevy with little tail wings that made it look like a compact rocket. She was a cheerleader and a class officer, but even without her other qualities, the '57 Chevy alone would have made her popular. She kept the car clean and wouldn't let any of the boys drive it, even around the block as they sometimes begged to do.

A new car stood out on our block; Larry noticed, and so did others. They noticed Kathy, too—her light brown ponytail hanging over the back of the seat. I had fantasized about her all semester, but in the flesh, in front of the house, I wanted her to disappear.

"I'll go get my book," I said. Under my breath I told Rocky to let her park. "It's only for a few minutes," I said, "and she'll stay in the car."

When I came out with my chemistry book, the hood was up

on her Chevy and Larry was peering at the carburetor and air filter.

"Your idling is way off," he said. "If I hadn't been looking, I'da thought you had a diesel."

"Forget it, Larry," I said. "She's gotta go." I gave her the book.

"It'll take me two minutes on the idle screw," he said. "You go to a garage, they'll keep it half a day and charge you twenty bucks."

"I did notice that it was noisy," Kathy said. "I thought it was just the wind."

Rocky came over to join us. "Don't let him touch your car," he said. "He monkeys with that piece-of-junk motorcycle all day, and even that never runs."

"I'm not charging," Larry said. "If she's not satisfied, she can take it wherever she wants tomorrow. Nobody's stopping her. This your car?" he asked.

"My parents paid for it," Kathy said, "but I drive it to school and wherever else I have to go."

"I'm available," Larry said, "if you ever need someone to ride shotgun, and I'll give you a ride on my convertible." He pointed to his Harley across the street. "Rocky's the only one who doesn't like her—I could sell her in a minute, but I never would."

He went across the street to get his tools. Rocky tried to lower the hood, but Kathy stopped him. "It's okay with me if he fixes it," she said. "It doesn't sound right. Maybe we can go over the chapter while he's adjusting the whatever-it-is. I don't know anything about cars, do you?"

"No," I said.

Larry returned in a minute with his tools in a rusty steel box. I knew more about cars than I admitted, but I stayed away. Larry took off the air filter and exposed the carburetor. Rocky looked over his shoulder.

"I'm not even sure what pages we're supposed to read," Kathy said.

I slid next to her on the front seat, closer than we had ever

160

been. I flipped through the pages in my book. The open hood gave us a little privacy.

I knew Rocky would leave us alone. He liked watching repairs of all kinds—plumbers, electricians, mechanics—he watched anyone who allowed him to, and though he knew nothing about the process, he didn't hesitate to offer advice.

Larry, at home with any engine, forgot Kathy and concentrated on her problem. "You ever had a tune-up?" he yelled. "The damn thing huffs like an old lady."

Rocky pointed to one chamber of the carburetor. "Why don't you unscrew this one?"

"If I do," Larry said, "she'll have to thumb a ride home."

"It's nice of your dad to do this," Kathy said.

"He's not my dad," I said. "He's . . ." I stumbled for the English word. When Gootie didn't call him "Bob," she used *paribok*, which was Russian or Polish for something like a serf who lived on your land. "He's a neighbor," I said, "and the older man is my grampa."

Rocky came out from under the hood. He stood at Kathy's window. He smirked. "What did I tell you," he said. "You let him start; now you'll be here all night."

Larry had removed the carburetor and the plugs; he cleaned the points. "In a half hour," he said, "you'll have yourself a free tune-up."

Kathy still thought she was getting a bargain. "I'm not in a hurry," she said. "Let's finish the chapter."

I had to invite her in. We sat at the dining room table—my regular homework spot. I pulled back the crocheted tablecloth. More than anything in the world I wanted Kathy to get in her Chevy and forget she had ever seen me, but I told her what I thought was most important about oxides.

When Gootie heard us, she came into the dining room. She assumed Kathy had come to see Maxine, since no girl had ever visited me before.

"Matkey downtown by Steketee's," she said.

While Kathy watched, Gootie opened a fresh bottle. She

served ginger ale as formally as waiters serve wine. She had a routine. Once she established that there were no chips on the top, she wiped the lip of the bottle with the hem of her dress. I had watched her do it hundreds of times and thought nothing of it, but with Kathy looking on, it seemed like something I had to explain.

"She worries that we'll swallow pieces of glass," I said. "That's why she checks the top of the bottle."

"I never thought of that," Kathy said. "I probably swallow glass all the time."

I knew about Kathy only that she had a car and a horse and mediocre grades on her chemistry quizzes. She sipped her ginger ale.

"I better see about my car," she said.

One of Larry's sons had joined him under the hood, a boy about twelve. They were almost done. Larry put the hood down quietly.

"Good as new," he said. "Start her up."

Kathy put my chemistry book beside her and started the car. She couldn't hear anything.

"It's great," she said. "Thanks a million."

"If I hadn't watched him," Rocky said, "he would have ruined it. Next time go to a gas station. Stop turning our street into a garage." He walked into the house.

I apologized.

"He's cute," Kathy said.

Chapter 21

I couldn't hide the girl, not after Gootie had seen her. Every day she asked.

"We're only friends," I said. "Leave me alone. Don't pester me."

"Friends," Gootie said, "that's a funny name for it."

"Stay out of my business," I warned her. "I can study with anyone I want."

"Fine," Gootie said. "I didn't know you call that studying. She sits there and licks her lips. I think there's something wrong with her tongue."

"I have no privacy in this house," I said. "If this keeps up, I'm moving out."

"That's what I was afraid of," Gootie said. "The girl knows what she's doing. She wants you to move out."

"She's doing chemistry," I said. "She's in my class. People study together all the time."

"How come you've been in school since you were five years

old and all of a sudden you need a partner to study? In Serei every boy studied with someone else, but with another boy, not a girl. She laughs like a monkey every time you say something."

"Is it a crime if she thinks I'm funny?"

"No," Gootie said, "she's right. You are funny. You're missing something up here"—she pointed to her head—"and here, too"—she pointed to her eyes. "Did she tell you she's pregnant yet?"

I decided to stay calm. "No," I said, "did she tell you she was?"

"She doesn't have to tell me," Gootie said. "I've seen it before. You think it never happened in Serei? The girl is pregnant; now she's got to find someone to marry her. Probably the boy is a good-for-nothing, so she's looking for someone else, someone who she thinks will make a good living. She picked you, and if you keep sitting there with her while she makes with her tongue and laughs and throws her hair all over the table, you'll end up with a lot less privacy than you have now."

I stood up to leave. "She's not pregnant," I said. "She's not trying to marry me, and even if all this were true, it's still none of your business."

When Kathy showed up for our next chemistry session she didn't know she was undergoing a pregnancy test. Gootie played the role of nice old lady, which Kathy thought she was. She filled the guest's ginger ale glass to the top and added a plate of egg *kichel*. While Kathy licked the sticky sugar from her fingers, Gootie checked for swollen ankles and bags under the eyes. Kathy thanked her. She talked in loud, slow phrases as if Gootie were a deaf child. I asked Gootie to leave the room. She motioned for me to follow her to the kitchen.

"Leave us alone," I said. "Stay out."

"Ask her if her mouth's dry," Gootie said, "and if she feels nauseous every morning."

"I'm not asking and she's not pregnant. If you don't stay out, we'll leave."

I went back to chemistry, and when Gootie returned to the dining room carrying a plate of grapes, I slammed the book shut.

"I can't work with all these interruptions," I said. I took the plate to the kitchen and threw the grapes into the garbage.

"She's not bothering me at all," Kathy said. "She's just trying to be nice."

"She's eavesdropping," I said.

"I thought you said she doesn't speak English."

"She doesn't," I said. "She catches a word here and there, but the way she keeps barging in bothers me."

"We could study at my house," Kathy offered.

I accepted on the spot. Kathy said she could pick me up and drive me home.

Gootie turned pale when I told her. "That's the end," she said. "If she's not pregnant yet, this will do it."

"And it will be your fault," I said. "You drove us out of the house."

"She's desperate," Gootie said. "Don't stay alone in a room with her."

"I wish you were right," I said. "She doesn't want me. She could have any boy in the school."

"And I know why," Gootie said. "Anyone can see why. The other boys run away. They're afraid, but you, you don't know anything about girls. She'll have you in a minute—honey, dear, sweetheart . . . She'll rub against you and you'll have as much sense as the cat. Where will you put her? You think your grampa will let her stay with you upstairs? Maybe you can convince him that she's not a girl—he doesn't know much, either—but once she has the baby it will be too late."

"She's sixteen," I said. "She doesn't want to marry anyone for years."

"At sixteen," Gootie said, "lots of girls in Serei got married or already knew who they were going to marry in a year or two. You told me that some girls in your school got married, even last year."

"They were different," I said, "not girls like Kathy."

"Probably smarter," she said. "They didn't need anybody to show them what's in the books."

The move to Kathy's house freshened my hopes. In our dining room with or without Gootie in the room, Kathy was interested only in chemistry. In another setting I hoped things might change.

"Don't go," Gootie said. "I'll leave you alone. I'll even go outside."

I refused her offer.

"In her house," Gootie said, "the first thing you'll see is Jesus on one wall and the Virgin Mary on the other. Maybe her parents already know about her; maybe the priest has kicked her out of the church. She told them about you with your face in a book, someone who doesn't know his mother from his father, and they decided, 'Well, even a Jew is better than leaving her the way she is.' Don't go," Gootie said again. She had talked herself almost into a panic. "It's a trap."

I enjoyed rubbing it in. "I'll go tomorrow," I said, "and any other time that she asks me to go, and if you don't give me privacy, I'll always go to other people's houses."

"This is an emergency," she said. "Don't go alone. Take him." She pointed to Rocky dozing in front of the TV.

The more she convinced herself that I would be walking into a sexual trap, the more I wanted to go.

"This is how it happens," Gootie said. "You aren't the first and you won't be the last. It's usually a boy just like you. They get him interested in a girl, sometimes she's even a witch, and as soon as he sleeps with her they come in with the holy water, sprinkle him, and take him right to the altar for a wedding."

"I'll make them wait," I said, "so you can be there."

"You think it's funny," she said. "That's all you know is funny. If you go to her house, you'll see what funny is."

Kathy dropped by to ask if we could study at her house in the evening instead of after school. "I've got riding at four," she said. "I don't mind coming to pick you up after dinner."

I told her I'd think about it. I didn't want Gootie following me out of the house. Even though I knew I could escape, the scene would be too humiliating.

I mentioned to Gootie as casually as I could that Kathy didn't have much time to study after school.

"Does she have a job?" Gootie asked.

"She rides horses."

"Like a Cossack," Gootie said. "They used to ride through the neighborhood with their whips in their hands in case they met a Jew. One of them hit Eserkey once and broke three of his ribs—for no reason—because he was walking in the street."

"Stop it," I said. "Have you ever heard of a Cossack in America?"

"I've never heard of anyone who rides horses in America. Here everybody has a car. She's got one. Why does she need a horse?"

"Lots of people ride horses for pleasure."

"Tell me one other person," she said, "who would jump on a horse and call it a pleasure. Maybe she thinks it will shake the baby loose."

Kathy came to my locker to give me her message. "I canceled riding," she said. "I decided that chemistry is more important."

She drove fast. Once we got beyond the industrial area all I saw were new one-story houses surrounded by lawns. I hadn't even been in this part of Grand Rapids. The broad lawns reminded me of cemeteries. Kathy did seem unusually friendly. She kept the radio on and moved her head to the music—half dancing, half driving. I carried my chemistry notebook and, in my pocket, the pack of Trojans.

Her house looked new and didn't seem to have enough furniture. I didn't believe anything Gootie told me, but I did expect a portrait of Jesus with a bleeding heart. I had seen such pictures in many other homes. Kathy led me into a den with a fireplace.

"We can work here," she said, "or in my room."

"Here is fine," I said. I hoped we would end up in her room. On the wall above the fireplace, instead of Jesus I looked at the mounted head of a deer, its antlers like a chandelier.

"Is your dad a hunter?" I asked.

"Yes," Kathy said, "but my mom got Clyde." She laughed. "We call him 'Clyde' because he looks like a Clyde, doesn't he?"

She served Coke and pretzels. "We don't have ginger ale," she said. "Sorry."

I put the Coke to my lips.

"You didn't check for broken glass," she said.

"I don't do that," I said. "Only my grandma does."

"I started doing it," Kathy said. She ran her finger over the top of her bottle.

In her own house she was distracted. She kept getting up to turn on the stereo, to make a quick phone call, to check for something in the clothes dryer. We were alone in the house. She seemed calm, but I wondered if she was nervous, too.

I felt as if Gootie were Clyde, watching us from the wall. Kathy had just started to copy what she needed from my notebook when we heard a car in the driveway. I saw a station wagon.

"It's Mom," Kathy said. She went to the door.

"We missed you," her mother said to Kathy. "It was a great day. The turf was dry."

She was slightly shorter than Kathy and looked hardly any older than her daughter. I tried to imagine her gunning down Clyde. She wore riding pants. I had seen Elizabeth Taylor in such an outfit, but never anyone in person. The trousers puffed out between her hips and her knees. They made her seem misshapen. She shook my hand.

"Kathy tells me you're a chemist-to-be," she said. When she swung open the kitchen shutters the late afternoon sun blinded me. "You can study in here," she said. "There's more light."

I was happy to leave Clyde. In the kitchen a wall plaque read "Cooking sticks, loving don't." As soon as Kathy finished copying what she needed she said we could go.

"Come again," her mother said, "or better yet, come to the stables with us. Do you ride?"

"No," I said.

"Kathy can teach you," her mother said. "You ought to make

a deal—chemistry for riding. She's really good. Did you see her trophies?"

"Mom," Kathy said, "stop it."

When Kathy dropped me off it was almost dark. I saw Gootie looking out the window. I put my books on the kitchen table and said nothing. Gootie held a dishrag in two hands. Her eyes were moist.

"I read psalms," she said.

"And we read chemistry," I answered.

"What else?"

"As far as I know," I said, "she's still without child."

"Don't joke," Gootie said. "Tell me what went on there."

"The same thing that goes on here, only there we drank Coke and at her house it's much nicer and quieter and nobody interrupted us."

"Were her parents there?"

"Her mother came in," I said, "just before we left."

"I knew it," Gootie said. "Were there other witnesses?"

"They expected the pope," I said, "but he was called away at the last minute."

I stopped when she pulled out her big white rag to blow her nose and wipe her eyes. On the table I noticed one of her green prayer books. She had a matching set of six. Two of the books she used for Rosh Hashanah and Yom Kippur. I knew they contained the standard prayers, but instead of a translation of the Hebrew into Yiddish, Gootie's books contained a bonus—a commentary written especially for women. She showed me what she had been reading. The pages had gone beyond yellow; they were brown and brittle. I sounded out the Yiddish until I recognized the phrases, but there were too many Hebrew words for me to understand the entire passage.

"It's Torah," Gootie said, "right here. This is what happens. If you don't believe me, look."

She had located the commentary about the biblical vigilante Pinchas, an ancient zealot who drove his spear through a fornicating couple. As far as I could tell, Gootie's women's book brought that event from Moses' era up-to-date. I stopped teasing her. The book was not something she referred to casually.

I knew how powerfully the stories affected her. On Rosh Hashanah and Yom Kippur, the only times she came to the synagogue, she was often in tears as she read her tragic and melodramatic commentary while the rest of the congregation was busy dispassionately praising God. That Gootie had gone to her books showed me the extent of her fear.

"Bring her back here," she pleaded. "I won't say anything, even if she goes with you into my bedroom. Just don't go back to her house."

I refused to promise. I knew that Kathy had a boyfriend and no interest in me other than homework, but in Gootie's melodramatic version, the girl desired me so much that a little bit of that desire did leak onto me. I started to look for signs. Gootie's fears had fueled my fantasies.

While she prayed and I carried the pack of Trojans, a third party intervened. Miss Pershbacher, the assistant principal, summoned me to her office. Kathy had spread the word about my tutorial ability to the chemistry teacher. He recommended me for a delicate job.

"We want you to do something very special," the assistant principal told me. She had been one of my mother's teachers, and she regularly confused me with my sisters. But as I sat in her office and she beamed at me, I thought she knew who I was.

"Since you're so good at explaining chemistry," Miss Pershbacher said, "we're going to let you tutor the colored boy."

I knew whom she meant. There was only one. He lived in the south side of Grand Rapids and came to school on a city bus. He wore round tortoiseshell glasses with lenses as thick as a hand.

"He's only here three days a week," Miss Pershbacher said, "for our special vision program, but he's taking regular classes as well. This is not an easy assignment," she said. "We thought long and hard about whom to ask, and . . ." She held out her arm, pointing to me even though I was the only one in her office. "You'll have your own room," she said, "just like a teacher. You'll both be excused from study hall. You'll be doing him a very great favor," she said, "and this will go on your permanent record."

At home my family was just as proud. My mother repeated to Gootie the phrase "just like a teacher." Gootie remained unimpressed.

"They're telling you that you should study with a boy," she said. "That's what the school wants, the same thing I want. You can bring him home all you want—black, white, I don't care who he is."

"I'll still be helping Kathy, too," I told Gootie. "This is just something extra."

Miss Pershbacher brought Willy Brown into room 332. I would reign for one hour three days a week in a room that had been my ninth-grade homeroom. Miss Pershbacher held Willy by the fingers and guided him to a desk.

"Our vision program is opening Willy's eyes," Miss Pershbacher said. "Now you can help to open his mind. A great task lies before both of you."

Willy was tall and very thin, slightly stooped at the shoulders. "I'm ready," he said.

I had prepared for our first meeting; so had Willy. I quizzed him on the periodic table—he took off his glasses, closed his eyes, and recited the table. When I gave him a few sample problems to test him on atomic numbers, he put his glasses back on, kept his face close to the page, and did all the problems in a few minutes. I checked his answers.

"You don't need any help," I said. "You got all the problems right."

"That doesn't matter," Willy said. He quoted Miss Pershbacher: "The colored boy needs help."

"I'll tell her that you don't," I said.

He laughed. "It won't make any difference to her. If you don't do it, they'll assign me to someone else. Around here a colored boy isn't supposed to be able to do chemistry."

Willy and I traded tales. As a Jew, I had the opposite problem. I had to fulfill the stereotypes of cunning.

171

"As soon as I joined the yearbook staff," I told Willy, "Mrs. Ennis made me become the business manager."

Before the end of our first hour we were friends. I even told him briefly about Kathy and Gootie. He thought he knew who Kathy was, but he wasn't sure.

"I'm okay close up," he said, "but in the hall all I can see are three thousand white faces zooming past."

After our meeting I steered Willy toward Kathy's locker so I could introduce my tutees to one another. Kathy canceled our session.

"I've got to ride," she said. "I'll see you later."

She canceled the following week, too, and finally she told me why. "I'm not gonna study with you anymore," she said. "Everybody says you're a nigger lover, and they're calling me one, too." The word and the phrase were conventional speech at Union. Kathy said "nigger" as easily as she might have asked me what time it was.

"Who would you rather help," she asked, "me or the blind kid?"

"He doesn't need help," I said. "He's better in chemistry than I am. And he's not blind."

"Then why are you doing it?"

"I'm supposed to," I said. "I'm his tutor."

"But you don't have to do it," Kathy said. "You can tell Miss Pershbacher you don't want to do it anymore."

At every session with Willy I thought about her. At home, Gootie asked from time to time where the girl was.

"She understands chemistry now," I said.

I didn't want to talk about it, so I didn't argue when Gootie announced her own conclusion. "She's in a home for unwed mothers," she said. "Thank God you escaped."

I felt less fortunate. Willy and I spent our sessions playing blackjack and poker. He was the only person I could have talked to about Kathy, but I didn't want him to know why she stayed away.

We skipped out of tutoring one day at eleven so Willy could

make a quick visit to my house. I had described everything that would happen. His vision wasn't good enough to see Gootie when she pulled out the special cup for strangers from under the sink as I'd told him she would, but he laughed when he heard the cabinet under the sink open. Gootie was so happy to see me anywhere near the lunch hour that she hardly paid attention to my friend. She started to bring out food for both of us. Rocky told us to get back to school before the truant officer arrested us.

He proved himself a prophet. There was no truant officer, but a few weeks later Miss Pershbacher herself caught us playing poker. We told her the cards were a visual aid, but she didn't buy it. Both of us had to go to the principal's office.

I bore the brunt of the blame. I should have known better. Each of us tried to provide an excuse for the other. I admitted that Willy was a terrific chemistry student, but as he predicted, Miss Pershbacher merely switched him to a new tutor. For my punishment, Miss Pershbacher kept me out of the National Honor Society. The principal informed my parents.

"A gambler," Rocky said. "Why shouldn't he be? Look what he sees."

The posted list of honor society members showed my name crossed out. I was also dropped from the tutor list. The notoriety helped my reputation. After weeks of staying away, Kathy dropped over to commiserate. It was a warm spring day; she wore a halter top and shorts.

"Don't let her in the house," Gootie told me.

When I let her in Gootie refused to serve her ginger ale. Kathy didn't understand the words, but she could read Gootie's looks.

"I guess she doesn't like my top," Kathy said. "It's so hot, though."

I told her not to worry about it, but I didn't want her to stay. If Rocky came in and saw the outfit, I knew he'd throw her out of the house. Gootie didn't leave the room. She stood at the doorway, lifeguarding me from temptation. Kathy giggled. This time she did flirt. Gootie and I both noticed. She laughed, and when she made a phone call she wound the long telephone cord around herself.

She put her chemistry book on the table the way she always did and then looked over my shoulder. I tried to concentrate, but I could feel Kathy's eyes on the book. Gootie warned me in Yiddish that the devil was at my back, but it was too late. Kathy leaned her head against mine. Gootie watched every move. Kathy knew, but she didn't care. She had nothing to lose.

"I'm failing chemistry," she said.

When she placed her hand on my shoulder, I trembled.

"*Kurveh*," Gootie said. Then she tried her English: "Hoor."

Kathy didn't understand. She was too distressed about her grade to pay attention to Gootie. "I need help again," she said. "I shouldn't have stopped studying with you."

None of us moved. Gootie broke the silence. "Hoor," she said again.

"Leave us alone," I told Gootie in Yiddish.

"No," Gootie said. "She's starting to show. Look at her belly."

"I just can't do this stuff," Kathy said. "None of the answers I get come out right, and I'm really trying."

"She wants to take you away in her car," Gootie said. "Don't go. If you're alone with her for ten minutes, she'll tell a judge and that will be the end of you."

"What's she saying?" Kathy finally asked. "Is she mad at me?"

"Don't pay any attention to her," I said.

Kathy gave me her most pleading look; her lips formed "please"; her eyes, for the first time, promised more.

"She'll tell you 'honey, dear, sweetheart,' today," Gootie warned me, "but she'll be a curse the rest of your life."

"Will you help me?" Kathy asked.

I shook my head. "I'm not a tutor anymore," I said. "If you need help, why don't you ask Willy."

Chapter 22

While I was still angry at Gootie for saving me from early fatherhood, she asked me to help her with a far more complicated love problem.

In Florida, after more than forty years of marriage, Yachey decided that she'd had enough. She found a doctor who listened to her three times a week.

"Come home," Gootie told her in a phone call. "Thank God you're a healthy woman. You don't need a doctor three times a week."

"I'm not coming back," Yachey said, "unless he comes to Florida and tells the doctor he loves me."

Gootie called her brother. "Let her stay," Leo said. "Tell the doctor to send me the bill."

Yachey used a new word. "What is this 'desire'?" Gootie asked me. "That's all she talks about."

I tried to explain.

"She's an old woman," Gootie said. "It must mean something else."

Gootie hated to use the telephone, but she talked to Yachey. During one call she handed me the phone. Yachey was laughing a little and talking fast.

"Tell her," Yachey directed me, "that it doesn't mean just to sleep with someone. I want him to talk to me. I want him to sit upstairs at the dinner table. I want him to treat me like I'm the mother of his four children, and when I told the doctor about his women, the doctor told me I should stay in Florida forever."

When Gootie phoned Leo time after time he had the same answer: "Let her stay there."

Gootie finally decided to intervene in person. I drove her to Alma. We stopped after every curve in the road so she wouldn't feel dizzy. It took us three hours to drive ninety miles.

Leo waited for us outside. When we drove up he opened his electric garage door. "There's no food in the house," he said. "Let's go to a restaurant."

We transferred to his Cadillac for the two-minute drive to the Big Boy. Gootie and her brother both wore grim expressions. I told her in advance that I was only the driver; I was going to stay out of the discussion.

She started slowly. "How long have you been married?" she asked.

"A long time," Leo said.

"How long?"

"I don't keep track," he said. "She does."

"After so many years," Gootie said, "wouldn't you miss a dog if the dog went away?"

"Dogs don't live that long," Leo said.

He parked and ushered us into the only fast-food restaurant in Alma. People were in church clothes, eating their Sunday dinners. The hostess greeted Leo by name and led us to a big table.

"Is she the one?" Gootie asked.

Leo ignored her.

When the waitress came to our table she too said, "How are you doing, Leo?"

"Yachey was right," Gootie said. "All these years I told her it wasn't true. Now I'm seeing it with my own eyes."

Leo addressed me. "Take your grandma to Florida," he said. "They can talk to each other. I'll pay for your tickets."

"That's all you know how to do—pay," Gootie said. "You can't pay to forget your wife."

"I'm paying her doctor two hundred dollars a week," he said.

"You're throwing away your money."

"I know that," Leo said. "Tell it to her."

"She doesn't need a doctor," Gootie said. "She needs you. Go to Florida and bring her back. That's all she's asking."

"As soon as I do that," Leo said, "she'll think of something else."

"Did your father leave his wife?" Gootie asked. "Did your grandfather?"

"I'm right here where I've always been. I'm gonna stay here till I die. She's the one who went away."

"Between a man and his wife there are no secrets," Gootie said. "Tell her everything."

"I can't tell her anything," Leo said. "She tells everybody she meets. Every day she says she's calling the Internal Revenue or the FBI."

"Since you were seventeen you've been in love with her," Gootie said. "You wouldn't go to America without her."

"I don't remember that," Leo said.

"I remember," Gootie said, "and she remembers. You don't take a woman away from her family and then abandon her in Florida."

"That was sixty years ago," Leo said. "There was no Florida then."

The waitress, a middle-aged woman in a short black dress, returned. Gootie glared at her.

"Ice cream for all three of us," Leo said.

"Let me know if you want anything else," the waitress said.

"I understood that," Gootie said. "I heard her."

"They all say that," Leo said. "They're supposed to say that."

"Which woman is it?" Gootie asked. "Show me." She looked at the waitresses, the cashier, the short line of people waiting to be seated.

"You want to know the truth," Leo said. "You pick—go ahead, pick any woman in here. I'd rather be married to any woman in the restaurant." He left the table and walked toward the cashier.

"He's lost his mind," Gootie whispered to me. "The demons have gotten to him."

Leo and I ate ice cream. Gootie let hers melt on the plate.

"Who can eat," she said, "in a place like this."

On the way home she hardly spoke.

When Yachey called that night Gootie wouldn't come to the phone.

"Is she sick?" Yachey wanted to know.

"Yes," I said. It was almost true. When Gootie didn't talk she was sick.

The rest of the family treated the Yachey-Leo split as a comedy. My sisters thought that Yachey going to a psychiatrist was the funniest thing they had ever heard, but for Gootie the whole earth rumbled. She believed that our dead and Yachey's ancestors, some of whom she'd known in Serei, were all counting on her as they had throughout the marriage.

"And I can't do anything," she said. "With him it's always like talking to a wall, but for more than fifty years she listened to me, and now, all of a sudden, she finds a doctor who tells her things doctors shouldn't even talk about."

I hadn't translated quotations from her doctor's lips for more than a week when Yachey surprised us. She arrived unannounced with four large Samsonite suitcases. She and Gootie hugged one another and both broke into tears.

"I came back for you," she told Gootie, "not for your brother, who shouldn't go crazy from the diseases he catches from his women."

We had no room for all Yachey's clothes. She couldn't unpack. "It's all right," she said. "I'm not staying—I only came to see you. Next week I'm going back to Florida. I'm the boss. Whatever I want I can do."

"She'll go back to Florida," Gootie whispered to me, "like I'll go back to Serei."

Yachey stayed at our house, and negotiations began. Leo would only talk on the phone after work, and Yachey wouldn't speak directly to him. She spoke to Gootie, who handled the telephone as if it were a grenade about to go off if she kept it too close to her ear. Every time Yachey tried to hang up it was my job to protect the connection.

Gootie was negotiating a reconciliation, but it sounded like a divorce. Yachey demanded in writing 50 percent of everything.

"She has it," Leo said. "Believe me I wish she didn't, but it's true. Every wife has fifty percent of everything her husband has. It's the law."

"I don't want it from the law," Yachey said. "I want it from him."

Leo agreed. He would give her 100 percent of everything she already had. He put it in writing. Matters of the heart were harder to settle.

"I raised four children; I lived forty-two years in Alma," Yachey said. "He's like a king there; he's got the junkyard, the Big Boy, the Rotary Club. You should see how he gets all dressed up to go to Bay City, where he gives money to the blind Lions Clubs. I don't have anybody, not a soul, and even when I go to Saginaw he drops me off in a store and says, 'I'll pick you up in two hours.'"

Twenty years before I heard of feminism, I recognized the flame in my great-aunt. The English words "desire" and "fulfillment" and "equality" came from the doctor. The Yiddish words "I'm seventy years old and lonely as a stone and he doesn't care if I live or die" came from Yachey. She wanted to assert that she had not lived in vain. She demanded from her husband recognition, not jewelry or fur.

"He wants free love," she said. "I want equal love."

"She can have any love she wants," Leo said. "Let the doctor give it to her."

Gootie considered it such an emergency that she even used the phone on the Sabbath. Leo wanted to send a driver; Yachey demanded that he pick her up.

When he finally agreed to do so, Leo dressed for the occasion. He wore a gray suit with his diamond Shriners pin on the lapel. Yachey, at seventy, still looked girlish. Had she known how to apply the makeup she used, she could have been called elegant.

Yachey waited in my sisters' room. We cleared out of the bathroom early to give her as much time as she needed to get ready. She wore a hat with a veil that came over her eyes. Gootie attended her. They spoke in whispers.

Leo waited outside beside his Cadillac. He leaned against it, as patient as a parking lot attendant. Gootie came out to greet him. He bent for her kiss.

"You're a *yoz* and an ox," she told her brother, "a fool and a stubborn man, but thank God you're here."

The Cadillac barely attracted a crowd. On Sunday at just past noon the street was almost empty. The stock-car racer and his wife, a redhead from Finland, were cleaning the dirt from number thirty-four, which he'd driven in the Speedrome on Saturday night. Some of Larry Hayes's children were chalking the sidewalk, and the Walizewskis, a Polish couple as old as Gootie and Rocky, sat on their porch with their blind collie, as they did every Sunday.

The bells from Saint Ann's Church were ringing and all the factories were closed when Yachey stepped out of the house. She wore pumps, Florida style, that showed her open heel and her painted toes. Gootie in sheepskin-lined house slippers and a dress that covered her elbows and her neck bones looked like her mother.

"Lashkey gonif," Yachey whispered loudly enough for all of us to hear. They had not seen one another for six months. She walked slowly down the stairs. Gootie held her hand in case she changed her mind. Leo didn't approach; he kept the car between them until she had descended and crossed the sidewalk. Then he hurried to the passenger door and opened it for her. They didn't smile; they didn't kiss. He kept the windows closed and the air conditioner off to please her.

We watched until the car turned the corner.

"Do you think she'll stay?" I asked Gootie.

"She never left," Gootie said, "but my brother wasn't smart enough to know it."

Chapter 23

*I*n my final year of high school, Gootie and I both had my career in mind. Her Max had worked in a store right after his graduation—then gone on to open his own. That store was still there in her imagination. What early death had stolen from him, she wanted for me. I knew what the store looked like: waxed wooden floors, a brown big-bellied cash register with round keys, three aisles, a dressing room for women, a storeroom in the back.

"In a few years," she told me, "you'll be a rich man. You'll wear a suit with a vest and you'll have a gold pocket watch with a chain."

"If I ever have a store," I told Gootie, "it will be a print shop. I'm going to be a printer." I had explained movable type to her before, but she didn't take my ambition seriously until I had the opportunity to begin an apprenticeship.

I knew that she didn't like the idea of my working in a shop. She made no distinction between a skilled trade and an unskilled one. I tried to present the nobility of printing through its finest example, Benjamin Franklin.

"He was a printer," I told Gootie. "He helped start America. He discovered electricity, and he was George Washington's friend. All his life he was a printer."

"Maybe that made his grandmother happy, but it doesn't give me any pleasure," she said. "I don't care about George Washington or King Sobieski, or Count Pototski. That was a long time ago. Did the man make a living?"

"He made the whole country," I explained. "He traveled all over the world giving people advice, he wrote books, everybody knew he was a great man, and on his tombstone there was just one word: 'Printer.'"

"On his tombstone," Gootie said, "it should say when he was born and when he died. That's what tombstones are for."

"He wanted everyone to know what his job was. He was proud of being a printer."

"To me," Gootie said, "it looks like he was ashamed to put anything on the stone. He was probably a schlepper."

"He was no schlepper," I told her. "Benjamin Franklin was a rich man."

"Did he own his house?"

"He owned a house and the whole building where he kept his printing press." I started to imagine Benjamin Franklin as a man out to impress Gootie. I gave him a few tenants like my uncle Joe; I stressed his qualities as a landlord more than his statesmanship.

"It sounds like he was a smart man," Gootie admitted. "It's too bad he never opened a store."

I spent half of every school day in the Union High print shop. Mr. Moeller had convinced me to major in printing. In the morning I took the academic courses, and in the afternoon I began my apprenticeship.

Rocky approved. This made Gootie immediately suspicious. "You'll end up like him," she said, "working all night for twenty dollars a week."

"Printers don't work nights," I said, but she caught me. I had bragged about all the money printers made on the newspapers.

"They must work all night," she said. "The paper comes in the morning like bread and milk."

Whenever I began to extol printing, she called me "Paper Boy."

I chose printing because it seemed masculine, unlike debate and speech, my sisters' specialties.

I defended printing to Gootie the way I always defended America. In fact, printing combined with Ben Franklin made everything the rest of my family did seem European.

"If not for printing," I told Gootie, "there wouldn't be books or newspapers or magazines."

"And even if there were no books or papers or magazines," she countered, "people would still need a jacket in the winter and underwear and socks."

Gootie's vision of a store had no chance against the print shop that Mr. Moeller offered.

Until I announced that I was going to work after school at a print shop, nobody in my family took printing seriously. My parents assumed I'd go to college like my sisters, but Mr. Moeller had turned my head.

"College boys don't earn what Linotype operators do," he said.

"If you want to be a printer," my mother said, "go to college first, and then be a college-graduate printer."

Rocky supported me. "It's a good trade," he said. "You'll never be out of work." He even knew the shop where Mr. Moeller told me I could be an apprentice. When they had parties or special events they always ordered a cake from the American Bakery.

I told Mr. Moeller I would take the job.

"You won't be sorry," he said. Moeller wanted to outdo the big major, auto shop. "The auto shop hot shots will have beer bellies and grease under their fingernails," he told me, "and you'll have money in the bank."

Gootie told me I was a *kuni lemel,* Yiddish for someone who is an easy mark.

"If you start up with this printer," she said, "you'll never leave. It will be just like the way you started with the reading. You put your face in a book and you forget everything. You'll look up one day and you'll be forty years old and you'll say, 'Yoo-hoo,' but it will be too late. Everybody will be gone. You'll be an old man sitting with a printing machine. In a store you'll be happy—there are always people, always something new."

I pointed out to Gootie everything that was printed—the words on the Instant Ralston box and every other label, the FOR RENT signs—but even surrounded by print she wouldn't change her mind. I told her about machinery that made newspapers, the great rotary presses I had seen only in movies, the kind that turned out the headlines.

"The only machine you'll need if you have a store," she said, "is a cash register."

"Benjamin Franklin never worked in a store," I said, "and neither will I."

I read Benjamin Franklin's diary aloud to Gootie. I pointed out how well organized he was.

"I tell you to work in a store," she said, "and all you can talk about is someone from George Washington's time. A store is modern. You can be modern, too."

On the side of printing I had, along with Ben Franklin, Glen Moeller, with his thinning red hair and his knowledge of what he called the real world. I spent two hours a day in his print shop. I could run a simple automatic press, and I knew the history of printing from the Gutenberg Bible to 1837, the date the first press entered the state of Michigan.

Moeller had been calling me "squirt" or "shrimp" all year; he had cruel nicknames for everyone. "This is what it's like in the real world," he reminded us. "You get a job in a machine shop or on an assembly line, it doesn't matter if it says 'Earl' or 'Gus' on your shirt—if you're fat, people are gonna call you 'Fatso.' This is how it is everywhere."

He evaluated me. "There's not much you can do," he said. "A

good wind would knock you over. You'll never get a job where there's any steel handling, and as far as construction goes"—he gave a gruff laugh—"you can put that outta your head, too. You were smart to choose printing. Size doesn't matter when you're at a Linotype—even a squirt like you can do fine as a printer."

Mr. Moeller admitted that he had no respect for education. "What are they learning upstairs," he said, "civics, home economics, American history? . . . I studied all that, too. Believe me, there's nothing better than printing."

Gootie considered him her enemy. "What if he told you to be a soldier?" she asked. "Would you go around with a gun? What is he to you? He's just a teacher."

Mr. Moeller had me scheduled to work at All Right Printing. The job would take up part of the school day. I'd earn school credits even while getting paid.

The wages I would earn didn't convince Gootie. "This is like throwing newspapers on porches," she said. "A store is a life, not a job by the hour. Work in a store. See if you like it—if you don't, you can always go back to the printing factory."

To humor her I read the want ads. We did find an ad for a store job, a tuxedo rental store.

"It's destined," Gootie said. "You looked in the paper and there it is."

"I'm not even going to call," I told her. Instead I made a list— like Ben Franklin. My first day at the print shop would be an entire day. At six I woke up. I shined my shoes. I made sure that I had lunch money and exact change for bus fare home. I double-checked the address of All Right Printing. At seven I left for work; I felt proud that I would be doing something that nobody in our family had ever done. I was going to be a printer.

Glen Moeller might have been the jerk that everyone in our class thought, but I had learned something in his print shop. I learned that I loved to put words together. Holding the steel stick in front of me, I did just what Ben Franklin had done. I composed in hard type, in lead. I learned how important a period was. The tiny dot required two thick slugs to follow it, and the paragraph with slugs on all sides, sat on the stick like an island.

Because my tray lacked small-case *l*'s I stayed away from adverbs. I could fit only nine lines on a stick, so I tried to make every word count.

With my shoes shined and my curly hair as combed as I could ever get it to be, I left for work early in the morning, the way my father did and Rocky did, the way the men in the furniture factories did. I had never felt more like a man and more like an American.

I was a half hour early, on purpose. I had read *Poor Richard's Almanack*. When the foreman of All Right Printing arrived he let me follow him into the shop, but he'd never heard of me.

"We don't have any openings," he said. "Moeller must have got it wrong." He took my name. "If anything turns up," he said, "I'll call you, but don't hold your breath."

Chapter 24

Gootie didn't rub my nose in it. She didn't have to; her prayers had been answered. I was working in a store, but she didn't understand rentals.

"Who rents a suit?" she wanted to know. "Even the poorest man saves until he can afford to buy one."

I brought home a tuxedo shirt to show her the nature of formal wear. She admired the ruffles and the French cuffs.

"I like this," she said. "Rich men in Odessa would walk around in clothes like this, but even there it was old-fashioned. No wonder nobody wants to buy."

She advised me to watch the boss and learn everything I could. "It's an opportunity of a lifetime," she said. "Keep your eyes open; see what he buys and sells; watch how he talks to the customers. Who else at sixteen gets such a chance?"

I kept my eyes open, and all I saw was trousers. On Monday morning I entered to face "the pile"—returned tuxedos from many of the weddings in western Michigan, all in a tangle on long wooden tables. It took me two full days to work through the pile, and I hated every minute of it. My only consolation was the radio. In the gloomy basement, surrounded by hundreds of black suits, white jackets, and tails, I measured inseams and listened to Elvis, Bobby Darin, and the Shirelles.

Rocky liked my hours: nine to nine, five days a week. "That's a day," he said. Before I went to bed I had to spend a few minutes telling Gootie about the store. I knew that she waited all day for me to report on "business."

"I don't know anything about the business," I told her. "I measure pants; upstairs they sell clothes. It's about as interesting as collecting rent."

"You don't understand," Gootie said. "Your boss started with used clothes, too. When he sees that you're ready he'll let you sell the new clothes. Tell him you want to learn."

I hated measuring waists and inseams so much that one day I did ask. Eric, the owner, said he liked my initiative.

"You want to learn the ropes," he said, "that's good." He used the phrase all the time when he checked on how I was doing with the pile. "Are you learning the ropes?" he would ask.

I nodded, but in the basement there were no ropes, only lengths and widths. The men's store upstairs carried flashy expensive suits, pointed-toe Stetson shoes, items like twelve-carat-gold-filled cuff links. Everything was overpriced. A big sign on the wall said "EZ Credit."

A dark, jowly man in his late thirties, Eric kept an electric razor in the bathroom. He checked himself for stubble every hour or so. "If I look like I need a shave," he told me, "don't be embarrassed to say so."

I never told him, and I don't think anyone else did. We didn't need to. We could hear the buzz of the razor every day after lunch.

"The ropes upstairs," he said, "are more complicated. If you were staying on, of course I'd want you to know about retail, but for the summer . . ."

"Quit school," Gootie urged me when I told her. "You can always go to school. If you stay in the store and learn everything you can, in five years you'll have your own store. No matter how much you study you'll never have your own school."

"I'd like to learn whatever I can," I told Eric.

"We'll see," he said.

"It's settled," Gootie said. "He'll treat you like a son. But don't tell him you want your own store. If he knows that, he'll throw you out."

Rocky liked hearing about the store, too. When I described measuring the waists and inseams for hours, his hands were itching. He had nothing to do. I waited for the right moment, then I invited him to come to work with me.

One Monday morning we walked down Division Avenue toward the area's bars, restaurants, and Andrew's Men's Wear. At the entrance to the basement Rocky looked through the smoky window at the pile.

"I could clean it all up in a couple of hours," he said. "Let me give you a hand."

Eric had gone to Traverse City for a week, and I knew that nobody would be checking up on me unless there was some kind of tuxedo emergency.

"You can try it," I said, "but it may be too hard for you."

His eyes narrowed. "Too hard for me?" he said. "This isn't even work. This kind of thing you can do after work."

I gave him a tape measure and turned on the radio. He gave me a look and shut it.

"No noise," he said.

After I put a packet of one hundred empty hangers on the iron hanging bar to get him started, I went to the women's area to explain. There was no way to hide him from Lee, the seamstress. At the other end of the basement her sewing machine faced the pile.

Lee did alterations and rented gowns to brides and bridesmaids. From her I did learn some of the ropes of bridal wear.

"I've been married three times," she said, "but the second one shouldn't even count. I bought a dress every time and shoes—the

190

whole thing. I'd never do it again." Lee always had a pile of tuxedo pants next to her blind stitcher.

"Eric hates bridal wear," she said. "He wants every woman to wear exactly the same thing, like the penguin suits."

She took special orders. If a girl came in early enough, she could get almost exactly what she wanted.

"Sure the dress might hang for six months before anyone rents it again," Lee said, "but it's already paid for—he hasn't lost anything."

"Space," Eric said whenever he came down to check bridal wear. "There's no place for the damn dresses."

He wanted to collect a large deposit against stains. "One spot and you might as well burn the whole thing," he said.

Lee refused. "Girls are careful," she said. "They don't go to weddings to drink beer and fight. They want to catch the bouquet."

I told Lee my plan to let Rocky work all week while Eric was gone.

"A week of measuring," she said, "after that he'll want to retire again."

Rocky ignored Lee when he hurried over to ask me for more hangers. "I haven't got time to stand around and talk like you do," he said. He grabbed his hangers, gave me a dirty look, and went back to the pile.

"One thing," Lee said, "please keep him out of the bridal area—the girls are nervous enough."

Instead of twelve hours, we finished in eight. I let Rocky do most of the work. When I tried to help he told me to get out of his way. I brought him coffee twice. He drank it in a few gulps each time, boiling hot. He refused any food. On the bus ride home he told me he felt better than he had in months. He ate his usual lunch at dinnertime, watched the news, then went to bed.

Gootie thought I was making a mistake.

"He'll steal your job," she said. "He doesn't care if they pay him or not. Don't let him talk to the boss or he'll say they don't have to pay you either."

Tuesday morning he woke me at six-thirty. He was ready. I told him that if he didn't let me sleep until eight, I would never take him again. Tuesday he did stop for lunch, a soft-boiled egg that he brought from home and mopped up with a slice of bread.

"I wish he could run the sewing machine," Lee said, marveling at his speed. "If he could do the bottoms, I'd have some time to expand the dress business."

She did the next best thing. Since I had nothing to do while Rocky worked, she taught me how to alter the trousers. I stitched the first few together so that no leg could get through. Lee just laughed and sliced the thread with a razor.

"Everyone starts that way," she said. "Don't worry about it."

I checked every pair, and after a few hours I thought I had it down. I kept my hands out of the way and controlled the needle with a foot pedal.

Lee did the waists, Rocky raced through the pile, and I did the bottoms at the blind stitcher. It felt like the three of us were a team in a turn-of-the-century garment factory.

"You guys are terrific," Lee said. "Eric ought to hire Rocky, too."

I had already decided that I would wait a day or two after Eric came back before I suggested exactly that. I would casually let him know that I'd let Rocky work all week, that he was terrific and would gladly sign an insurance waiver or whatever else an eighty-five-year-old had to do in order to work.

Eric came back from Traverse City angry. He had caught a cold, and the fishing had been terrible. He shaved before noon.

"I'd stay out of his way today," Lee said.

I knew it without her advice. I had spent all morning explaining to Rocky why he couldn't come with me.

"If he doesn't like the work I did last week, let him tell me to my face," Rocky said. He packed his lunch.

To keep him from following me to the bus stop I had to

threaten to quit. "I'm not going," I said. "If you want to go alone, go ahead. You either let me try to arrange this the right way or I'm through with the tuxedo business and so are you."

When I left he was scrubbing the birdbath even though he had washed it the day before.

I needed his help, too. The pile was even bigger than usual. After a week of letting Rocky do most of the measuring and sorting, it felt awful to go back to the drudgery. I would rather have been at the sewing machine practicing my new skill and listening to Lee and an occasional bride.

In midafternoon Eric summoned me. "I've gotta go to the doctor and get something for my throat," he said. "You can watch the floor for a while."

Bob, his salesman, had gone on an assignment to arrange rentals through a men's store in Kalamazoo. I was the only one left in the store.

"If someone comes in," Eric told me, "let him pick what he wants, and if it's a jacket, you don't ring it right up. You say, 'How about this shirt? They look great together.' You understand?"

Eric told me to look around some before he left and ask questions if I wasn't sure of something.

"Is this marked right?" I asked about a pair of trousers that had a fifty-dollar tag.

"You think that's too much?" Eric asked. He walked away from the cash register to examine the pants.

"It seems like a lot," I said.

"How much do you think I'll actually get?" Eric asked.

"Fifty dollars."

He slapped me lightly on the side of the head. "In my dreams," he said. "Ten percent down, five dollars a week, until he loses his job or his wife takes everything in a divorce or he goes on a drinking binge or he just decides he's paid enough for the damn thing. Clothing is not furniture. Once he walks out onto Division Avenue, the next stop for the clothes is the Salvation Army store. After three months, the account goes to a collection agency, and they take most of what comes in. Which, believe me, isn't much. For that fifty I'll be lucky to take in twenty-five, and think of the heartache." He coughed and went to the bathroom to gargle.

When he came out, I told him my grampa was really interested in the work I did with the tuxedos.

I had put Eric in a philosophical mood. He walked around straightening the tags on a few sport coats. In spite of his cold he lit a Camel.

"A kid like you," he said, "you've probably never had a job before, right?"

"Not full-time."

"You come in here—you see the volume in formal wear—you think I'm rolling in money, right?"

"That's none of my business," I said. I didn't want to stir him up; I wanted the friendly, smiling Eric who could trade jokes with the groomsmen.

"I'm not gonna tell you this isn't a good business. It is. You've been here long enough to know that. But you have no idea of the losses I take in men's wear."

"Then why not just rent tuxedos?" I asked.

"The sixty-four-dollar question," he said. "Why not? I'll tell you why not. Don't ever quote me on this, but you know what a tux is? It's a uniform, just like the coveralls the guys wear in a gas station, a uniform for getting married, for going to the prom. We even sell a few every year for guys to get buried in."

I tried to bring the conversation back to Rocky. "My grampa," I said, "isn't that interested in tuxes. He just likes to clean up to make order. He'd be great working at the pile."

Eric ignored me. "You notice any junk here?"

He pointed at his fixtures—the glass cases with carefully folded shirts, the leather seats in the shoe department.

"I paid fifteen dollars a foot for the carpeting," he said. "Did you notice that everyone who comes to rent walks in the front door, passes by everything before he gets to the measuring area? Why not just have him walk into the basement the way you do?"

I shrugged.

"You don't get it. You think a guy wants to rent a wedding uniform in a basement or a garage or in a dingy store full of double-breasteds and suits with two pairs of pants?" He shook his head. "Christopholis, the Greek dry cleaner, rents tuxes—same price as I do. He has a little storage space, so he takes a flier—he even throws in dry-cleaning specials sometimes. You think he does any business?"

I shook my head.

"You're damn right he doesn't. Who wants to think about his girlfriend while he's smelling dry-cleaning fluid?"

I was taking mental notes for Gootie.

"You shouldn't have got me started," Eric said. "My goddamn throat is killing me. Stay near the register. Don't leave the store unless there's a fire. I should be back in an hour or two. You know what those doctors' waiting rooms are like." He ran a hand across his cheeks before he left.

After an hour without a customer I decided that working upstairs was even more boring than measuring tuxedo trousers. Then three men in straw sombreros entered.

"No English," one of them said.

I welcomed them with a memorized dialogue from my tenth-grade Spanish class. The men were delighted, and so was I. My first chance ever to use my Spanish. They wanted pants. I walked with them to the two rows of wool and Dacron and gabardine trousers in a dozen shades of brown, black, blue, and gray.

I could see that all three had waists less than thirty. In English I would have felt awkward, but their pleasure in my Spanish encouraged me to speak more. I rattled on like a border-town salesman. When I wasn't sure of a word, I came close enough for them to help me.

They wanted one pair of pants each. When I pointed out the dressing room the spokesman explained that they didn't need a dressing room. He demonstrated by making a fist, then putting his hand and forearm up to the elbow into the waistband. If it fit precisely across the arm, it would fit the waist. I wanted to try it myself, but there wasn't a pair of trousers small enough for my waist. We laughed together. I was hoping Eric would return in time to see how well I was doing as a salesman.

"What about the bottoms?" I asked. "You need to try them on so we can alter the bottoms—no charge." I bragged, "I can do it for you myself."

Their spokesman said the bottoms didn't matter; they would just roll them. I was trying to convince him that he had nothing to lose when Rocky walked in.

"I've been in the basement, waiting," he said. "What's the matter with you? The pants are all a mess downstairs, and you stand here talking."

I left the customers and tried to explain that the boss had ordered me to do this. I was more angry than he was. "Go home," I said. "I told you that you couldn't come back until I talked to Eric."

"I waited all morning," he said. "How long does it take to ask him?"

"He's got a sore throat. He went to the doctor. I don't want to bother him until he feels better."

"He'll feel better if he knows somebody is downstairs measuring the pants and hanging them up so it won't look like a pigpen."

I heard the freight elevator doors open. Lee stepped out and motioned to me from the rear of the store. I left Rocky and the Spanish speakers and walked toward her.

"I tried to get up earlier to tell you he was here, but I've had three customers. He's been pacing the floor. I finally had to tell him where you were," she said. "He walked in during a pinning. The girl was in a hoop and a bra. He said, 'What is this? A whorehouse?'"

Lee was laughing, so I knew she wasn't angry, but it made me even more furious. "I'm sending him home right now," I said. "I don't even want to ask Eric to hire him."

When I returned to my customers Rocky was yelling at them in English.

"Dummies," he said.

I grabbed his arm and pulled him toward the door.

"Go home right now," I said. "They know what they're doing."

"Look at them. How can you sell them forty-dollar pants?"

The men were smiling. They seemed to understand that Rocky was my grampa.

"Union?" Rocky asked.

They shook their heads. The spokesman took out a check—made out to him. He asked for a pen to sign it over to the store. The check was for forty-eight dollars.

Rocky told me to ask him how long he worked to earn that forty-eight dollars. I hesitated, but when Rocky started asking in English, I asked in Spanish.

"A week," he told me. We began to talk. I translated for Rocky. The men were migrant workers. This month they were harvesting onions and radishes. The truck had dropped them off and would pick them up, he said, in an hour. Andrew's was the first store they'd seen, so they'd walked in and were delighted to find someone who spoke Spanish. They didn't want to miss the ride back to their farm.

"Take them in the basement," Rocky said, "and give them each a pair of pants. The ones that you told me to hang in the back."

Trousers that held a spot that didn't come out or had begun to unravel at the black stripe or needed work on the waistband we hung separately. Sometimes, when we ran out of stock, we did use them, but usually they were extras.

"I can't give away anything," I said, "and neither can you. It's not our store."

"You told me those pants aren't good anymore. They just hang there. Why shouldn't they wear them?"

"They're damaged," I said.

"So what? They don't need forty-dollar pants to work in the fields."

The customers didn't know what we were arguing about.

Rocky led them to the back of the store, but he didn't know how to operate the freight elevator. I followed and tried to explain in Spanish that they shouldn't listen to him; he didn't work in the store.

The spokesman held up his check.

"The money is good money," he told me in Spanish. He didn't understand why I wouldn't take it. He was carrying all three pairs of trousers.

The men followed me back to the sales floors. We left Rocky pushing the elevator buttons with no success.

"*Camisas?*" I asked, and pointed them toward the shirts.

In a minute Rocky stormed past me carrying three pairs of damaged formal trousers. The men put their forearms into the waistbands.

I took the pants back. "Not for sale," I said.

"They're not worth anything," Rocky said, "but they're just as good as what you're ready to pay forty dollars for."

One of the men told me he didn't like the formal stripe on the side.

"You see," I told Rocky, "they know what they want."

The other two men gave me identical forty-eight-dollar checks.

"If you sell them those pants," he said, "I'm not going to work here."

"Good," I said. "Go home."

He walked out the front door. Before I rang up the sale, I asked them if they knew about any other stores. They said they didn't. I told them the pants they chose were very good but very expensive; at Sears just a few blocks away they could find much lower prices. They only had an hour, the spokesman said. They didn't know where the other stores were.

Rocky had gone outside, but he stood in front of the store, his face pressed against the glass. I motioned for him to come in.

"Will you take them to Sears," I asked, "and get them back in less than an hour?"

"In ten minutes," he said.

I tore up the receipt and rehung the trousers. I folded the frayed formal pants and put them on the freight elevator.

"Any customers?" Eric asked when he returned.

"No," I said.

"Too hot," he said, "and I've got a temperature when it's ninety outside."

Rocky, followed by the three migrant workers, walked in. The workers were wearing new cotton trousers. The tags were still on their waists, and their cuffs were rolled.

"Seven dollars," Rocky said to me.

Eric greeted the group as customers.

"What can I show you gents?" he said.

"Are you the boss?" Rocky asked.

Eric nodded.

"You should be ashamed," Rocky said, "to charge forty dollars for pants." Each of the workers shook my hand and then left to await their truck on the corner.

"What's going on here?" Eric asked.

I told him.

"You mean," he said, "that you sent three customers to Sears when they were ready to buy here?"

I nodded.

"Who's paying you a buck an hour?" he said. "Me or Sears?"

I apologized, but I told him the men needed work pants, not dress clothes.

"I was going to go home and leave you here the rest of the day," Eric said, "but I see that I can't trust you."

"Ask him," Rocky said. I tried to signal Rocky to leave, but he stood his ground.

"My grampa would like to work downstairs," I said. "He's good at measuring."

"I can do it one, two, three," Rocky said.

"That's your job," Eric said. "Or are you too busy sending people to Sears to do your job?"

I didn't say anything.

"Well," Rocky said, "you want me or not?"

"No," Eric said, "one person downstairs is plenty."

Eric never let me set foot on the sales floor again. He began to check closely on the way I packed shirts and cummerbunds. He stopped sending me out to buy him coffee and cigarettes.

"I wouldn't work in a place like that anyway," Rocky said. "I was just doing it for a few days to help you out."

Chapter 25

Levinsky, one Saturday afternoon, took time out from Torah study to brag about his granddaughter. "A real beauty and smart as a whip—she's like me, not her father."

Sol Lee, the onetime appliance, tire, and toy merchant, had gone on to greater things. He owned a statewide brake-store chain. "The only time I see him," Levinsky said, "is on the television. Every few weeks he calls up. He says, 'Pa, do you need anything?'

"'I need a son with as much sense as money,' I tell him. 'I'll see you soon,' he says. 'I've got a busy schedule. I'm not even in town most days.' 'Who cares?' I tell him. 'When you're here you have nothing to say anyway—just brakes and tires.' That's all he knows. But Suzanne, his daughter, thank God, takes after me. She's refined. She's marrying a doctor."

"If she's like you," Gootie said, "that doctor's only problem will be sickness."

"Don't worry," Levinsky said, "your granddaughters will get married, too."

"I'm not worried," Gootie said. "If yours could find someone, we see God at work."

Rocky interrupted. He'd had enough of idle talk. He led Levinsky upstairs for their regular study session.

"At her wedding," Levinsky said, "you'll see quality people, a wedding like you've never seen. There will be three hundred people; money is nothing to Sol."

Every week Levinsky added wedding news. His source was the bride herself. "She calls me from Philadelphia, Pennsylvania," he said, "just to see how I feel."

"She's looking for business for her husband," Gootie said.

"He's not a doctor yet. He has two more years," Levinsky said, "and he won't have to look for business. People will run to him."

"Two years is a long time," Gootie said. "By then maybe Moshiach will have come and there won't be sick people."

Levinsky talked about the wedding until our invitations didn't come. "I don't understand it," he said. "I'll give you mine." He handed Gootie a thick envelope. He had scratched out his name and written "Yerachmiel and Gootie." Gootie didn't have to read to understand.

"Your son thinks we're not rich enough to come to the wedding," she said. "How rich do you have to be to be able to buy her a few towels or a set of sheets?"

"I'm giving five hundred dollars," Levinsky said. "That's enough to pay for anybody I'll invite."

Rocky said he didn't need any invitations. "If I want to go somewhere, I go," he said. "Do you think I've never been to the Pantlind Hotel?"

"So come," Levinsky said. "You don't need a map and you don't need this." He pocketed his invitation.

"If Sol doesn't want us," Gootie said, "we're not going. We're not schleppers. We've got plenty to eat at home."

"Bring them," Levinsky said to me. "I'll get you an invitation, too."

"We'll wait until she has a baby," Gootie said. "Then we'll come to the *bris*. For that you don't need a hotel and an invitation."

Nothing changed until the week before the wedding. At the end of August Levinsky arrived for his study session with a guest. Even dressed in a Penn T-shirt and blue jeans, she looked like a bride. She had blue-black hair, and she leaned to kiss Gootie and Rocky. She shook my hand.

"What did I tell you," Levinsky said. "Is she beautiful or not?"

Gootie admitted it.

"I'm so sorry about the invitation," Suzanne Lee said. "These things just happen when there are so many details."

I translated for Gootie.

"The only detail that matters," Gootie replied, "is the husband."

"The husband is fine," Suzanne said, "and we both want you to be there. Grampa's friends are important to us. That's what I came to tell you."

"There you have it," Levinsky said. "You think she goes to everybody to beg them to come?"

"I hope you'll be there," Suzanne said. She put a long arm around Levinsky and kissed the top of his bald head. "If he's not happy, I won't be happy," she said.

"I don't go to weddings that start eight o'clock at night," Rocky said. "I go to bed."

Gootie just shook her head. "Tell her I'm going to get her the best sheets there are—one hundred percent cotton, a top and a bottom."

Suzanne looked genuinely disappointed. Even when she pushed out her lower lip like a child, she still looked beautiful. "I'm counting on you," she said to me. "Will you be there?"

I couldn't say no.

"The invitation is open for every one of you," she said. "I hope they'll change their minds."

"They'll change," Levinsky said. "Nobody wants to miss a wedding like this."

At the reception, as I stood among strangers, I was angry at Gootie and Rocky, but even more so at myself for promising the bride I'd be there. I kept my eye on Levinsky, waiting for the crowd of well-wishers to thin so I could shake his hand to let him know I had kept my word.

He looked great, his pink face and head contrasting with a white dinner jacket. I was relieved that his suit fit. He had asked me to measure him so he wouldn't have to go downtown to Andrew's. I went to his house with a tape measure. He was a thirty-eight short, but he insisted that he was a forty-two regular.

"Put down what I say," Levinsky told me. "I know better than your ruler."

"It will be too big," I warned.

"Too big is okay; too small is trouble."

Before I placed the order for him I checked with Eric. When I read out Levinsky's waist, inseam, and chest, Eric told me what to do.

"Thirty-eight," he said. "He probably does need a short, but give him a regular so it will be too big and make him happy."

"He told me he wants only a forty-two," I repeated.

"Then tell him it's a forty-two," Eric said. "How's he gonna know?" Eric told me a trade secret. "That's why we take the labels out. We go by fit, not by number."

I ordered the thirty-eight for Levinsky as Eric suggested, but I worried all week that he'd find out it wasn't a forty-two.

When I delivered the suit, Levinsky apologized. "Look what my rich son did." He took me to the hall closet to show me a new tuxedo. "He bought it—thrown-out money," Levinsky said, "and a shirt and cuff links and this little girdle, the whole package." He tried on the cummerbund for me. He wanted me to show him how to wear it.

"It's a beauty," I told him.

"How much does a suit like this cost?" he asked.

"I don't know," I told him. "We don't rent any like that."

"A hundred dollars?" he asked.

"Probably more," I said.

I could see that he enjoyed looking at himself in the mirror.

"I'll take this rental back to the store," I said, "but I don't think I can get you a refund."

"Get yourself one," he said. "Tell them I said to rent you one."

I did. The tuxedo was optional for guests, but as long as I had a free one I wore it. It also seemed like the right way to end my summer at Andrew's and my brief career as a store worker. Although I had measured thousands of tuxedos, this was the first one I'd worn. As I looked around at all the other men in tuxes, I couldn't stop estimating their waists and inseams. I didn't know any of the wedding guests.

"Are you a relative?" someone asked me.

"A relative of a friend," I said, "the grandfather's friend."

"It must be an old friend, then," the man said.

"Since 1919," I answered.

The man raised his plastic champagne glass. "I'll drink to that," he said.

Although their primary connection was the Saturday afternoon study session, Rocky had sometimes visited Levinsky during the week. A few times he'd even asked me to drive him to what Levinsky called "the shop." Surrounded by a golf club factory and a tool-and-die maker, Levinsky's business looked more like a cluttered backyard than a shop. He had one employee and one piece of equipment, a shear that hadn't cut anything in decades.

Levinsky bought mostly from peddlers, the kind who arrived with the trunk of their car held open by a piece of rope. He bought the brass in plumbing fixtures and auto radiators, the lead in batteries, the cast iron in bathtubs. He wore a cap with a brim, a blue workshirt, and hunting boots. At his shop he was all business. On one of our visits Rocky had tried to suggest a job for himself.

"I'd clean the place up," Rocky said. "I'd put everything in order."

"You'd drive away all my customers," Levinsky said.

"Customers," Rocky said. "You call them customers? They steal a few pieces of pipe on Saturday night and sell it to you on Sunday."

"If they steal, they have to sell it somewhere else," Levinsky said. He pulled out a stained ledger that looked like something a nineteenth-century clerk would have used. "I write down everybody's name and ask where the property came from. The police come sometimes and look at my book. 'A crook would have to be nuts to sell to Levinsky'—that's what the police say."

"In one day," Rocky said, "you wouldn't recognize this place."

"It's a junkyard," Levinsky said. "It doesn't have to be clean. Go clean the bakery."

In the middle of the ballroom the bride and groom were dancing. I envied the doctor-to-be. Suzanne reached out to her father. I had seen Sol in his TV commercials lots of times, but I would have recognized him from his bike-and-tire days. He had gray hair and a speckled mustache now, but his broad face hadn't changed. He danced with his daughter, and then she pulled Levinsky into the center of the dance floor. He tried to get out of her grip, but halfheartedly. The guests who were watching called out encouragement. When Suzanne wouldn't let him get away Levinsky put a hand delicately around her waist and waltzed Suzanne in a slow and courtly style. They looked like the top of a music box. When the waltz ended everyone cheered and Levinsky bowed, not to the crowd, but to his grandchild. She kissed him.

It was so lovely that I was glad Gootie wasn't there to be jealous, as I knew she would be next Saturday when Levinsky recounted the event.

At the bar a few teenagers were telling the bartender that he looked like Floyd Patterson, who had briefly been the heavyweight champ. I tried not to stare, but they were right. I wandered over to order something just so I could have a closer look; then I heard a woman scream. The crowd closed in on the dancers. The groom held Levinsky's head in his lap. People were yelling for someone to call an ambulance.

The Floyd Patterson look-alike shrugged. "Happens at every wedding," he said. "Someone gets drunk and passes out."

In a few minutes the ambulance came and I caught a glimpse of Levinsky, still in his white dinner jacket, being carried out. The bride was crying; Sol entered the ambulance with him. People were telling one another that he'd be all right. The excitement was just too much for him. The band tried to get people in the mood for celebrating, but nobody returned to the dance floor.

Levinsky's family disappeared. The band leader took the microphone.

"Folks," he said, "we're all scared—I know that. But Sol wants everyone to have a good time. Come what may, the band plays on."

He tried a rhumba number, then "The Tennessee Waltz," but everyone was leaving. People said good-bye to one another quietly. I saw someone writing a note on a napkin. I stayed because I didn't know what to do. Like the other guests, I was worried about Levinsky, but I also worried about Rocky and Gootie—she would be waiting for a report on the wedding.

I stayed until the band packed up, hoping there would be a message from the family. Then I drove to Butterworth Hospital, directly up the hill from the hotel. Rocky and Levinsky had walked that hill together every Saturday. They would stop at the bus stop benches so Levinsky could rest.

In the emergency room I sat between a man with a deep cut on his hand and a feverish child who cried continuously no matter how much his mother cooed to him. I wanted some news about Levinsky before I went home. The clerk would give me none.

"Only family can get any information," she said.

I had a good idea what that meant, but I didn't want to believe it. I stayed in the emergency room because I didn't know what to tell Gootie and Rocky. After about an hour I saw Sol walk through the electronic doors. Suzanne was behind him, crying against her husband's shoulder.

I walked toward them. Suzanne saw me. She shook her head, and they disappeared into Sol's car.

Chapter 26

*R*ocky came home to rest before the funeral. He sat up all night with the body; then he washed Levinsky and helped the undertaker dress his friend in a burial shroud.

"He wasn't sick," Rocky said. "We're burying a healthy man. It was just time for him to die."

Gootie was less stoical. She spent most of the morning crying quietly in her room. When she came into the kitchen she tried to convince Rocky not to be a pallbearer.

"Let the young men carry the coffin," she said. "You prepared the body. You don't have to put him into the ground."

"If they'd let me," Rocky said, "I'd dig the grave, too. Even dead, Levinsky knows more than the young ones do."

The funeral at three P.M. Sunday was like a continuation of the wedding. The out-of-town guests were there, and when I drove Gootie and Rocky to Sol's house after the funeral, I recognized the wedding food still on the caterer's trays.

Gootie whispered to me, "Don't eat anything."

"Why?"

"I don't know," she said, "just don't."

"Nobody poisoned him."

"I'm not saying that. It just doesn't feel lucky to me. None of this does. You go to a wedding and it turns into a funeral. Who knows what can happen in such a world?"

Above the fireplace in Sol's living room hung the portrait of Levinsky. Sol had borrowed it from the synagogue. Gootie smiled. "That he would have liked."

When Sol noticed us he hurried over. He put his arms around Rocky and sobbed.

"Stop crying," Rocky said. "Everyone should have a death like his."

"You're right," Sol said. He hugged Gootie and spoke to her in Yiddish. "I knew what you meant to my father," he said. "All these years, every Saturday . . ." Sol spoke Yiddish to me, too, and he led all three of us to a group of important-looking people.

"These people were my father's best friends," he said. He introduced us as if we were the guests of honor.

"Look at this one," Gootie whispered. She recognized Dan Samuelson, a city councilman. "The pipe looks like it's part of his mouth."

We had seen his picture in the paper lots of times. His mother sat behind us in the synagogue on the High Holy Days. He came too every year for a token appearance. Always surrounded, the councilman obliged everyone who wanted a word and a hand-shake. Whenever I pointed out his picture in the paper or told Gootie that I'd seen him on a local news show, she had only one comment: "If he wasn't so famous and he had a wife and children, he'd be better off."

Sol led us right to the great man. The councilman shook Gootie's hand and kept talking to the people on his right.

"Such is life," he said. "People come and go. What can we do?"

"Ask him," Gootie whispered to me, "where his mother is."

"Mother is sick, nothing serious," Samuelson said. "Just a cold, but as you get on in years even a cold isn't just a cold."

"Say hello to her," Gootie had me say.

"I will do that," the councilman said, "and I'm sure she'll be sorry to have missed you."

"These people," Sol said, "without people like my dad and them, there'd be no Judaism in Grand Rapids."

"There isn't anyway," Rocky said. "Let's *daven mincheh*. I didn't come here to eat and talk to big shots."

"You're right," Sol said. He started to pass out prayer books and called people into the living room for the brief service. He asked Rocky to lead everyone in prayer.

"A big mistake," Gootie said.

Rocky finished before many people had even found the correct page in their prayer books, but Sol couldn't get enough of Rocky and Gootie. He brought us to several other groups of guests, introducing Rocky and Gootie as "the real thing."

"If he likes us so much," Gootie whispered to me, "why didn't he want us at the wedding?"

I told her not to ask.

"I'm not crazy," she said. "I'm asking you, not him."

When we ran into the councilman for a second time, Gootie took my elbow and led me away. "I see why nobody married him," she said. "He's got a pipe. Why does he need a wife? Look at him. He doesn't take it out of his mouth for a second. If he didn't eat, it would be part of him forever. If I hadn't seen him before, I'd think he was the undertaker." Even while we sat across the room on leather chairs, Gootie kept her eyes on Samuelson. "Every few minutes," she pointed out, "he turns his neck. He's looking for his mother. He must be over fifty and he's still a mama's boy."

Rocky was anxious to leave. Sol walked us to the door. "When you're here," Sol said, "I feel like Pop is still around."

"He was around for eighty-five years," Rocky said, "but you were busy becoming rich."

"You're right about that, too," Sol said. He tried to hug Rocky again, but Rocky squirmed away.

In the car and later at home, Gootie didn't say anything. That night she asked me to come to the kitchen.

"I've been thinking all day," she said.

"We're all sad," I said. "I've been like that, too."

"I'm not thinking about Levinsky," she said. "For him there's nothing to think about anymore. He's in a good place. I'm thinking about Samuelson and his pipe and about you."

"What about me?"

"I'm afraid you'll be like him. You'll become a lawyer with a pipe, and you'll go everywhere with your mother."

"Or with you and Rocky."

"That's what I mean," she said. "I looked around at Sol's house. There were other young people there, but only you were with your grandparents."

"Are you just noticing that now?" I said.

"I'm thinking," she said, "that Samuelson was once a good-looking boy. I used to see him when he was your age. He'd wait outside while his mother went into the butcher shop. 'He doesn't like to look at meat,' his mother would say. 'He's going to be a lawyer, not a doctor.'"

"She was right," I said. "He did become a lawyer."

"He became a nothing," Gootie said. "His mother should have told him, 'You don't like the butcher shop, then don't eat the meat.' You think people really want to talk to him? Go on, all they want to do is get a close look to see how a man like that gets his picture in the paper so many times." She put the handle of her spoon between her teeth and pretended to tap tobacco down and reach for a light. She spoke English. "Mine mother hawt ah cold, eet's nahthing." She blew air out of her lips.

The next day Gootie retrieved from the back of the closet an almost empty pillowcase. She had tied a knot to keep the inch of loose down at the bottom safe. The pillowcase had yellowed in the twelve or thirteen years since I'd dropped goose down into it, but the knot she had tied was so strong that she needed my help to undo it.

"I thought there was more," she said. "There's not enough

here for a scarf. If you're going to college, you'll need a pillow. I'll buy you one," she said.

I showed her the list of supplies that the dormitory would provide. I pointed to the word "pillow."

"Rubber," Gootie said. "In America they all sleep on rubber."

Gootie and I had our own shorthand. She knew what baseball, which she called "*goyishe* pleasure," meant, and I knew what a pillow meant. The pillow we went to buy wasn't merely a place to rest my head, and it wouldn't be light. I would be carrying my ancestors.

In Serei, pillows mattered the way bread mattered, the way where you sat in the synagogue mattered and who your father-in-law was mattered. A pillow was a form of status. Gootie had no idea what a dormitory or what a college could be like. But whatever sort of place it might be, people would still look over your bedclothes. For her grandson she wanted the best. If heaven was like the Pantlind Hotel, then a good pillow was close to heaven on earth.

It was also another start on the even more important project. Gootie alluded to it as we walked through Steketee's Department Store. "Maybe we'll buy two pillows," she said, "and I'll save one for your bride."

We walked past some of her favorite stops, starting at the half-size shop where she bought dresses that were much too large until Miss Scofield, a spinster with hundreds of pins and time on her golden hands, made everything fit.

At housewares I thought Gootie would enjoy telling me how much better her own pots were. "No," she said, "I'm not shopping today. Today I'm buying you a pillow and that's all." We walked past millinery and men's. We didn't even glance at other departments, but at the border of shoes and boys', Mrs. Rood spotted us. She hurried over.

"That witch," Gootie said. "Let's go." Her mood changed. She tried to talk faster, but Mrs. Rood cut us off.

"I haven't seen you in the longest time," she said, "and look who we have here—Granny."

Gootie muttered "Granny" to herself.

I wanted to be polite. Mrs. Rood had been working in the boys' department ever since I'd been going to Steketee's. Gootie didn't like her because she asked too many questions. "You come to buy a shirt," Gootie said, "and you have to tell her how many children King Sobieski had."

I was sure Mrs. Rood's misshapen back aroused Gootie's superstitions. Bent by osteoporosis, the saleslady made a virtue of being able to place her face close to size and price tags. She could flick through stacks of Levi's jeans to pull your size in a few seconds.

Her interest in customers was unusual, but I thought it was okay as long as I wasn't in a hurry. She had sold me my bar mitzvah suit, my Davy Crockett cap, my Confederate army cap, and, many years ago when she met Gootie, the sheepskin winter jacket that Gootie came to inspect because it was on sale and couldn't be returned.

Mrs. Rood looked at me as if I were a movie star. "What a big, handsome boy you are now," she said.

I liked hearing it, but at five feet four inches I was big only to her and to Gootie.

"Er eez sick and er hat pimples," Gootie said.

Mrs. Rood understood "sick" and "pimples," and I caught on to what troubled Gootie. Mrs. Rood looking at me with such interest had raised the danger of the evil eye.

Certain people, Gootie thought, had the power to curse. All it took was envy. They couched the evil eye in praise, they admired you, and then they caused you misery. Because there were so many people at large who were capable of the evil eye, the best policy was always modesty. Gootie never wanted my clothes or my hair or anything else to be just right. Imperfection meant safety. Strangers paid no attention, so they were no problem, but someone like Mrs. Rood, who pressured you with questions, had to be avoided. She might be innocent, but why take a chance? I knew all this and tried to balance Gootie's superstitions with common courtesy.

"School clothes?" Mrs. Rood asked.

"College clothes now," I corrected.

"Well, well," she said, "how time flies."

Gootie tried to hurry away, dragging her leg as fast as she could. I waved and followed her.

"I was just being polite," I told her. "I'm not going to buy any clothes."

"Why did you have to tell her anything?" Gootie asked.

"It's not a big deal," I said. "Just forget about her."

We were almost in domestics when Gootie clucked in almost perfect English, "Well, well, how time flies."

I laughed, but she wasn't kidding.

"She's a witch," Gootie said, "and now you've told her that you're going to the *gemanazy*." She used the Russian word for college. "Don't be such a show-off," Gootie said. "I'm not even going to look at pillows if you start telling everyone you need a college pillow. If they ask, say you need a pillow because you've got a sore neck."

"Nobody cares why I need a pillow," I said. "I don't have to give a reason."

"You think people just go out every day and buy pillows?" she said. "Open your eyes. The store is full of clothes everywhere you look—pillows are only in this little corner. You don't go to buy a pillow like a pair of shoes; the salesladies know that. They'll ask you why and you'll start bragging and before you know it you can forget about going to college."

I thought I could tease her into a better mood. "You've got too much money," I told her. "That's your problem." I pointed to the pocket of her dress, bulging from the contents of a knotted handkerchief.

"Forget the pillow," she said. "I'm not buying a pillow for Todres, the village idiot. You think it's a joke to sleep on rubber. You think I carried the pillows and featherbeds across the ocean so you could make jokes."

She started to walk away from me, but the escalator trapped

her. She was afraid of it; she had to wait beside the moving stairs until I would lead her to the elevator.

I apologized and promised to be serious. I seated her in a chair, then one by one I brought pillows for her to lean her head against. After she finished she insisted that I take my turn. On the display bed we had a pile of duck down, goose down, down and feather, and total feather. Because the pillows all looked alike, I kept forgetting which was which, so we had to retry them all. We were the only customers in the department, so we could take our time. We were still undecided over an hour later when Mrs. Rood wandered over from boys', two departments removed. Gootie sat up straight and stopped testing.

"I put you on my list," the saleslady said, "of all my boys who have gone on to college. Over the years there have been dozens, and I'm proud of every one. I try to send all the college boys a Christmas card."

She handed me a ballpoint and asked for my college address.

"You see," Gootie said in Yiddish, "what did I tell you about her? Let's go."

She stood but didn't walk away. When I started to write she grabbed my arm.

"Don't give her anything. Spit on her," she said.

"My grandma doesn't feel well," I told Mrs. Rood. I pretended to support Gootie, but I really wanted to hold her arm to keep her from pushing Mrs. Rood away. We hurried to the elevator.

Our jovial mood had ended. I knew what might be coming. Once I had been with Gootie when we ran into Mr. Siegel, an old man with thick trifocals that made him look like a frog. Gootie claimed Siegel was the one who put the evil eye on her son, Max. Max had worked for him before opening his own store.

I was about ten when we saw Siegel unlocking the trunk of his car at a parking meter downtown. Gootie began to wail. She sounded like the Moroccan women I had seen in movies. Everyone on the sidewalk stopped to watch. Siegel looked at us. He closed his trunk. I didn't know if he understood that he was the monster in our lives. I hated him, too, even though he was a stranger to me. He didn't know what to do; neither did I. A few passersby asked Gootie if they could help. She stopped wailing. She spat in all four directions to ward off the evil eye. She grabbed my hand and pulled me close to her, as if Siegel might try to abduct me.

"May your heart be as broken as mine," she yelled to him in Yiddish. "May you know my sorrow." Her anger gave way to tears. She pulled a rag out of her pocket to blow her nose. Gootie had let go of me, but I stood next to her and could feel the sobs go through her body. If he had taken a step toward me, I would have spit, but Siegel only stared.

"Let's go home," I said. I tried to pull her arm, but her body was still heaving.

"Murderer," she sobbed, "you shouldn't walk on the earth."

Siegel didn't try to answer. He looked at me as if he wanted to say something; then he opened his door and drove away. The incident lasted only a few minutes, but it left a deep impression. Mrs. Rood, trying to be kind, had unlocked a bottomless pit.

I could feel Gootie's arm tremble.

"She's just an old lady; she doesn't mean any harm," I said. "If she wanted to curse me, she could have done it years ago."

"You don't know about these things," she said, "and may you never know." I led her to the small restaurant within the department store. While she sipped ginger ale I tried to divert her back to pillows, but her heart wasn't in it. We did return to domestics, using a different set of elevators to avoid the boys' department. I brought out all the pillows again. "You choose," Gootie said. "Whatever you want is good."

We didn't buy. That night, with both of us still sobered by the shadow of what had happened at Steketee's, Gootie took out her tools: the small scissors, the tweezers, and the hand mirror that she kept rolled in a soft washcloth and hidden with her money.

I walked in on her once when she was using those tools. She was embarrassed, but she told me the story. She blamed America, her sister-in-law Sarah, and herself. "It happened the first year that I came from Serei," she explained. "I was in Muskegon and

Sarah said to me, 'Gootkey, I have to tell you something. In America women don't go around like this.' She pointed to my chin. Under my chin I had a hair as big as a fingernail. Who knows where it came from or how long I had it. I never thought about it. As much as you think about your elbow, that's how much I thought about that hair.

" 'Cut it off,' Sarah said. 'In America they'll laugh at you if you don't.' She gave me a scissors, and I cut it. In a few weeks that hair grew back, darker and longer and with another hair beside it. I didn't understand what I had done—once you cut a hair you can start a hundred growing.

"I called Sarah in Muskegon. 'What shall I do?' I asked her. 'Cut them both,' she said. She was laughing. 'What a greenhorn you are,' she said.

"Thank God I didn't listen to her or I would have had a beard like a man."

The one hair over the years had grown to about a half dozen. Sometimes when Gootie waited too long you could notice a hair, but usually she kept them plucked to invisibility. She removed the hairs with a tweezers; then she applied witch hazel to her skin with the washcloth. She had been using the same tools wrapped in the same cloth since 1923.

"Sarah, may she rest in peace," Gootie said, "had a face full of hair. When she got old and her heart was weak she didn't care anymore."

For our surgery Gootie used these almost sacred tools. I held the ticking of her pillow with the tweezers so my fingers wouldn't touch the ancient down. We used a Gillette Blue blade to make the incision. Gootie didn't touch the down, either. She used the back of her hand mirror as a scoop. We shoveled some of the contents of her pillow into mine. It took a long time to fill the case, and as careful as we were, there was still down floating across the linoleum in Gootie's bedroom.

I offered to take the pillowcase to Andrew's store so that Lee could stitch it on the sewing machine, but Gootie refused.

"What if you drop it?" she said, "or a wind comes along and blows it away?"

I went to bed at one when she was beginning a second set of stitches to secure the interior of the pillow. She handed it to me the next day after work. A zippered pillow guard covered the hand-sewn pillowcase, and another pillowcase covered the guard. The new pillow was a third the size of the one I used at home and light as air.

"With a pillow like this," Gootie said, "you can sleep anywhere."

When Gootie brought the pillow into the living room to show it off, my sisters laughed at me.

"My roommate is allergic to feathers," Bailey said. "If I brought in something like that, she'd never stop sneezing."

Maxine warned me. "You're not leaving Serei and coming to America," she said. "You're just going a hundred and sixty miles to Ann Arbor. Don't bring that pillow or chicken soup or herring or anything else Gootie tells you that you'll need. If you start out that way, you might as well stay home."

I hid the pillow in the upstairs closet, where Gootie would never find it because the stairs were too difficult for her, but the pillow was on my mind when I said good-bye. She awoke at seven, the middle of the night to her. She filled a thermos bottle with coffee.

"Don't forget your pillow," she said. I nodded.

My father said we would leave at eight. Rocky had been pacing near the car since six-thirty. Every few minutes he came into the house to announce the time. We made a mistake by giving him a departure hour. When he had an exact time it was a countdown to liftoff.

By a quarter to eight I had yelled at him three times to leave me alone and Gootie had joined in, always happy to be against her husband's punctuality.

"I'll get there when I get there," I said. "It doesn't make any difference what time."

"To you," he said, "nothing makes a difference. What are you going to do when you have to punch a time clock?"

"He'll never punch a time clock," Gootie reminded him. "He's not like you; he'll be a boss. He'll come in whenever he's ready."

"He'll be a boss like your father was a boss," Rocky said.

Their exchange made me feel less lonely. As usual, the conversation ended with Rocky storming upstairs.

My father took our Dodge to the gas station to check the oil and tires. Bashy cooked in advance the afternoon and evening meals for Gootie and Rocky since she wouldn't return until very late that night.

Bailey was already working in Detroit; Maxine had gone to college a few days early to be with her friends. I was the last to leave. Nobody said anything about it, but we were all tense. Rocky was right—a quick getaway would have been the best thing.

My father was punctual, too. Rocky didn't have to oversee the time. At five to eight he returned, gas and oil topped up, tires at thirty-two pounds, even the spare. My father transferred his truck driver's sense of caring for the equipment to the car. He checked and double-checked everything. We also knew, because of Max's accident, that every trip was a dangerous one.

Gootie had stationed herself outside at the edge of the driveway. It was one of her standard observation posts. I could have marked it with an X, to the inch. Like the kitchen doorway or the bottom of the stairwell or her coffee-drinking chair, it was a spot where Gootie positioned herself. She wanted to be as close as possible to her stoves and refrigerator and still see the world.

My two suitcases had been in the car since the night before. Gootie didn't ask about the pillow, although I was prepared to lie. I was also prepared to leave and had hardened my heart. I was going to say good-bye and go off to college just like everyone else who wasn't tied to his grandparents. I had convinced myself that Ann Arbor was not the end of the world. There were letters; there was the telephone.

"There were letters and telephones," Gootie reminded me, "when I left my parents in Serei in 1923, but I never saw them again."

I didn't fall for that one. "I'll see you Thanksgiving," I said, "in three months." She had her big white handkerchief in the pocket of her dress, but there were no tears.

"God willing," she said.

While my parents waited in the car I went upstairs to say good-bye to Rocky. He had made the beds, dumped the waste-basket full of my last-minute junk, and put the books that I kept beside my bed into his bookcase. I hadn't even left the driveway and he had removed all traces of me.

"I'll call next Sunday," I said. "I'll call every Sunday."

"Do what you want," he said.

"I want to say good-bye."

"You said it."

"I want you to say it, too."

"Go on," he said. He looked at his watch.

"If you don't say good-bye," I said, "I'll be late for college and it will be your fault."

He gave me a hug and then a kiss with his bristly white mus-tache. I ran down the stairs and past Gootie, who stood like a security guard at her post. I didn't stop; I waved.

My first night in the dormitory I couldn't sleep on the standard-issue pillow. The second night I rolled two shirts and stuffed them into a pillowcase. When that didn't work I went the next day to a store in Ann Arbor to price a down pillow—almost twice the Steketee's price.

I phoned home on Wednesday, only three days after I left.

"I forgot my pillow," I told my mother. "Please send it, but don't tell Gootie," I said. "She'll make too big a deal out of it."

Chapter 27

*T*he handwriting on the envelope was my father's; the letter inside was from Gootie.

"Dear Mottele," she wrote in Yiddish and in pencil:

> Don't worry about *kashress* [keeping kosher]—eat. At the wedding canopy God forgives everything. Your grandpa has something to do. Sam lets him pull pieces of rubber out of some of the junk that comes from Kalkaska. He spends all day in the garage wearing a pair of gloves that are twice as big as his hands. When he comes in to eat or take a drink he expects me to salute him as if he's in the czar's army. "We're making ten cents more a pound," he says. He thinks it's a fortune. To your father it's just more to gamble away.
>
> We went to Alma last Sunday to the same restaurant where the waitresses should be ashamed

of how they dress. Yachey came too. Leo eats supper upstairs with her every day. She says that when
it gets colder he's going to Florida with her. I'll believe it when I see it.

At college don't be a show-off. If you're not so
smart it's just as good. Don't study too much and
never late at night or when you're alone in the
room. I'm glad you have a roommate.

One Saturday you know who came over?—Sol
Levinsky. He said he wanted to study with Rocky
like his father did. "You don't know anything,"
your grandpa said. "It's like studying with a don-
key." I gave him a glass of tea. He says he misses his
father and he's going to give more money to charity. I told him that coins are round—they roll
away. He looks older now and more like Levinsky.

Your cousin Rose sent your mother dresses
from New York. They're too big and she looks like
a streetwalker, but I don't say anything because she
doesn't have to pay for them. Rose works for a
dressmaker. I think they give her what nobody else
wants and then she gives what she doesn't want to
Bashy.

Don't forget to eat. Be well.

It took me a long time to read the Yiddish; then after I figured
out all the words I read the letter over and over.

Written words between us seemed as odd as singing to one another. I knew exactly where she was sitting as she wrote. I knew
that it was late, that her stoves had been wiped clean, that she
had checked the gas and the door locks before she sat down to
compose. She would use the same caution before she spread my
letter out on the table, smoothed the folds of the page with her
hands, and then began to savor the words.

I had a pen pal. In her second letter, which came a few weeks later, she told me that her brother Joe had come to visit with a woman.

"Here," the woman said, "I brought you a present." She gave me a box of strawberries. I don't know where he found her. It's been so many years since Sarah died and all of a sudden he shows up with this bundle. Write him a letter and tell him to be careful. She probably thinks because he has a safe she'll be rich. I told her he doesn't even have a freezer. She should think of that instead of the safe. Joe says she's a bookkeeper, an educated woman. Are you learning bookkeeping? Joe says that if you know how to do bookkeeping you'll always have a job.

I hope Joe finds a wife, but not her. She speaks so much English. She might even be an American. I didn't ask. When you come home from college tell us what you want to eat. Bashy says you'll want potato kugel, but that's not enough.

Be well.

For winter vacation some of my friends went skiing or they visited one another. I turned down invitations to Detroit and even one to New York. I took the early bus home on Sunday morning. By two o'clock I was ready to share my learning. On the bus I arranged my notes. A few hours after I got home, I began to give Gootie a taste of college. She removed all the dishes before I put my thick book on the table. I pretended I was the professor looking out at a packed auditorium. Gootie blew her nose and gave me her full attention.

"I'm not trying to change what you believe," I told her. "I'm just going to tell you what's true. You can believe whatever you want—we're going to talk about science."

She nodded. "Everyone wants to know what's true," she said.

"We're going to discuss evolution, how the world became what it is today."

Gootie leaned back in her chair as relaxed as if she had just come out of the bath. She had dressed for my arrival, even to the point of wearing her black shoes with a quarter-inch heel.

"The world is very old," I said. "There have been many changes in natural history." I had an immediate problem. There were no Yiddish words for the geologic ages, so I used the English words "Ordovician" and "Mesozoic" and "Cambrian," but I said them with a Yiddish accent.

She was impressed. "Such words," she said. "You have to be smart just to remember them."

I decided to switch to pictures. In the geology textbook I pointed to a graph comparing the age of the earth with the appearance of humans.

"If the whole history of the earth was squeezed into one day," I said, "people would only arrive at about ten minutes before midnight—that's how much older the earth is than people."

"I believe it," Gootie said, "but who told you this?"

I turned to a new illustration, a page of rock photographs.

"That's a good question," I said, "and the answer will surprise you. The history of the world is written in rocks."

She tried to hold back her laughter. I ignored her and went on with my lecture.

"Everything that has happened—the earthquakes, the volcanoes, the ice, it's all there in the rocks."

"So, in college," Gootie asked, "you look at stones, and from that you know about everything?"

"Not everything," I said, "but most things."

"In Serei, we had a woman, Rachames, who didn't even need stones. She could look at your hand or feel your head and tell you everything that had already happened and everything that was going to happen."

I rolled my eyes the way the geology professor did when someone asked a stupid question. I even answered the way he did. "My dear," I said, "apparently nothing is getting through."

Gootie said "my dear" back to me in English; then she laughed so hard that she had to go to the bathroom.

She returned with a new question. "If I looked at the stones in the driveway," she asked, "could I understand everything about the world from them?"

"No," I said, "you have to know where to look. A mountain is good, or a good riverbed, or a big deep canyon."

"Have you looked in such places?"

"No," I said, "you know I haven't."

She pointed to the geology book. "You looked here?"

I nodded.

"And whatever it says here you believe." She shook her head. "If this is what you're learning, maybe you should forget about college. We'll talk about the rocks later," she said. "Too much of this and I'll have to take headache pills."

I didn't let her get away. "This," I told her, "is the key to everything." I laid out, in straightforward Yiddish, the theory of evolution.

Gootie took it in without interrupting.

"I know this must turn the world upside-down for you," I said, "but there it is. It's what everyone believes now, and it's true. A man named Darwin figured all this out by studying turtles in South America."

"That everything changes," Gootie said, "a person can figure out without going to South America."

"It's not only that things change," I said. "It's the way they change, over millions of years, by chance. One animal develops a long neck, another an eye, another a lung; there's no pattern. The ones that are strongest live and have the most children."

"And the ones that don't have children," she said, "live at home with their mothers like Samuelson the politician. Does the book tell you the best thing is to get married and have children?"

"That's not the point," I said. "I'm not talking about people; I'm talking about everything—animals, flowers, insects."

"That's why the Torah is better than your book," she said. "In the Torah God talks about people. He doesn't have to tell flies to get married or to follow the Ten Commandments."

"Nobody's saying this book is like the Torah," I said. "It's just a schoolbook. There are thousands of books that explain evolution." I had to use a roundabout phrase for evolution: "How things came to be as they are."

Gootie turned a few pages in the book. "Did they pay someone to write this?"

"Of course," I said.

"How much?"

"I don't know," I said. "It doesn't make any difference."

"That's what you think," she said. "He's some wheeler-dealer, making money by telling you that rocks outlive people and that babies come from mothers. He's making money telling you things that were an old story to Adam and Eve."

"I'm going to have to start over," I said. "I didn't explain this well enough."

"You explained fine," Gootie said. "Someday you'll explain it to your customers."

We were still arguing when I saw Joe's Ford pull into the driveway. He wore his brown fedora, and the woman with him wore a round hat decorated with flowers.

"Did you know Joe was coming?" I asked Gootie.

"You never know about him anymore," she said. "He goes wherever the bookkeeper tells him to go."

Joe shook my hand. The bookkeeper hugged me.

"I heard a lot about you," she said. "Your uncle thinks the world of you."

"This is Marlene," Joe said. "She's an educated person, too."

"I graduated from Ferris Institute in Big Rapids," she said.

She was much younger than I expected, probably in her late fifties.

"Well," Joe said, "what do you think of her?"

"She's fine," I said.

"You're not supposed to ask while I'm standing here," Marlene said. "You wait until later. What do you expect him to say?"

She sat down across from Gootie, who tried to busy herself making tea. Marlene thumbed through the geology book.

"I'm not the world's smartest cookie," she said, "but I can read just about anything."

"Show him," Joe said.

Marlene pulled a pair of glasses out of her purse. "I buy them at the drugstore," she said, "but they're as good as an eye doctor's."

"She can see without them, too," Joe said.

"Scientist, huh?" Marlene asked.

"No," I said, "I just took one science class." I tried to keep talking to her because I saw Joe and Gootie whispering to one another in the dining room. Marlene was less interested in geology than Gootie had been.

"My first husband, may he rest in peace, was a jeweler," she said. "He talked about rocks, the expensive kind."

"Have you been a widow for a long time?"

"Twice," she said. "Never got over the first, and then it happened again. But life goes on."

"You seem like a cheerful person," I said.

"What else can you do? Talk about cheerful—your uncle over there, he's quite a card."

The card and Gootie returned to the kitchen.

"The way you make up your bed," Gootie said, "is the way you sleep in it."

"That's right," Joe said.

I told them I had to go to my room to read. Joe walked me to the stairs.

"Do you like her or not?"

"If you like her, I do," I said. "She seems like a nice woman."

"She wants to marry me," Joe said.

"Good," I said, "I'll come to the wedding."

Joe laughed. "I'm too old."

Later Gootie told me what they were whispering about. "I feel sorry for the woman," Gootie said. "He doesn't want to get married. He likes her because she's got a driver's license and can write

English. And she wants him because she thinks he'll die soon and leave her a lot of money."

"Maybe they should get married," I said. "They'll both get what they want."

"You went to college," Gootie said, "and you learned how rocks turned into people and you still don't know a fig from an onion. She wants a husband; he wants a driver. You think that's why people get married?"

"Did you say anything to her?"

"I'm staying out of it," Gootie said. "The woman has buried two husbands. You'd think she would look for a younger man this time."

We were at our familiar spot, the kitchen table, at our familiar time, after everyone else was asleep.

"I've been thinking all day about the rocks and stones," Gootie said. "You know the saying 'As lonely as a stone'? It's the worst thing that can happen to a person, to end up alone. Stones are alone. They don't talk; they don't feel anything. They stay in one place like the dead.

"Your teacher talks about stones because he wants you to learn that you shouldn't be like one. That's what it's all about. The turtles and South America is just monkey business. Forget about it."

Chapter 28

*B*y the time I was a senior I thought I spotted evidence of God's work on my behalf. I wanted to tell Gootie, but not too much and not too directly. I waited for the right moment.

"The fraternity is having a big party, the fiftieth anniversary."

"I'm glad they're happy," she said.

"I'm going to give a speech."

"You always give a speech."

"This is different. There will be people from all over the country. We're renting an entire motel. This year I'm the president."

"The cat is a president, too," Gootie said. "That's why she washes herself so often and other cats come from all over to the back porch. In America, who isn't a president of something?"

"Your husband's coming," I said. "Do you want people to think I only have a grampa?"

"He won't go," she said. "He told me he'd never go back there."

Rocky had visited once. He gave me a day's notice. When he stepped off the bus I went on to look for his suitcase.

"I didn't bring anything," he said. "All I need is a piece of soap and a towel." He had his tefillin and his tallis in the pockets of his jacket. I took him to the fraternity house.

"Are they Masons or Odd Fellows?" he asked.

The Odd Fellows was a lodge he had belonged to in the 1920s.

"It's a college club," I told him. "It's not the same, and don't ask people if they're Odd Fellows."

"There's nothing wrong with Odd Fellows," he said. "Philip was an Odd Fellow, Joe Post, most of the men at the bakery."

"All right, just don't mention them. It sounds funny."

"And to me 'Alph Bet Zeta' sounds funny. At least 'Odd Fellows' is a word."

He arrived about eight-thirty. I gave him a cup of coffee, then he marched to the attic dormitory. I slept in the bunk above him. He snored all night, and at five, when he woke up, I jumped down to keep him from waking everyone else.

"I'll help you work," he said. I was a waiter. I had to serve breakfast at seven. Rocky had everything on the table before five-thirty.

That night we walked to the synagogue, where there were fewer than the required ten for prayer. We didn't have ten next morning, either. When we returned to the fraternity house, guests were arriving for the pre–football game brunch. It was a cold but sunny day, football weather in Ann Arbor. Rocky sat in the dining room, reading from the Talmud that I had borrowed from the synagogue. He glared at everyone who came into the house. Whenever someone shouted, "Go Blue," Rocky said, "Go to hell."

"It's worse here than in Grand Rapids," he said.

At two, while I listened to the game on the radio, he went upstairs to take a nap. As soon as the Sabbath was over he took the night bus home.

Two years had passed since that visit, but I thought Rocky

would forgive and try a new adventure. He was always ready for anything. Not Gootie. She hadn't spent a night away from home since she came to America in 1923.

"Forty years," I reminded her. "Once every forty years can't you spend the night in a hotel?"

"Why should I?" she asked. "I've got everything here."

I told her there was a girl I wanted her to meet.

She looked at me as if I were someone else. "You're teasing me?"

"No," I said, "I want you to meet her."

"For an engagement?"

"No engagement."

"For no engagement I won't ride in a car all day. If it's only 'honey, sweetheart,' your grampa is enough."

When she came to the telephone a week later, I wasn't surprised by her question.

"Is there an engagement yet?"

"No," I said, "nothing has changed."

"Then I'm still not coming."

The following week she asked the crucial question: "Does her father have a store?" I knew then that she'd come to the anniversary weekend.

"He's a lawyer," I said. "He has an office."

"Maybe he has a store on the side. Ask."

"Lawyers don't have a store on the side."

"Why not?" she said. "If you can have a side business, why can't a lawyer?"

My "side business" was her great pride. As soon as I moved to Ann Arbor, I noticed that tuxedo rental prices were twice what they were in Grand Rapids. I also knew that Eric's vast inventory mostly hung on the basement racks until the June weddings began. During the pledge formal season I went to the fraternity houses, measured the renters, and had their tuxes delivered from Grand Rapids. The renters saved five dollars and Eric paid me two dollars a suit.

I hated the role I played, walking into a fraternity house during dinner, making my announcement, then pulling out my tape measure, but for two dollars a suit I was glad to do it.

Gootie couldn't hear enough about my work. Whenever I came home I brought my order book. Sometimes I read aloud to her the names and inseam and waist sizes of my customers just so she could enjoy the music of commerce.

"Now you're like a peddler," she said. "When you earn a little more you'll order your own suits." Since I was on my way, a bride was not out of the question.

"Ask her father," Gootie advised me, "where he's from."

"I know," I told her. "He's from Chicago."

"That's not what I mean. From what real city—Warsaw, Vilna, Minsk . . . ?"

I did ask Terry. She had no idea.

"He was born in Chicago," she said. "So was my mom." She knew that her ancestors probably emigrated from Eastern Europe, too, but to her that time seemed as remote as the Civil War.

"If she doesn't speak English, how am I going to talk to her?" Terry asked me. "Does she speak French or Spanish?"

"She knows prices," I said. "You can say things like 'a dollar ninety-eight.'"

"I'm serious," Terry said. "We could have a real communication problem."

I didn't know how to explain that Gootie understood what mattered without understanding the exact words.

"Is she psychic?" Terry asked.

"Maybe she is," I said. "I never thought about that."

"I don't believe in that sort of thing," Terry said. "She'll have to convince me."

For the fraternity's fiftieth anniversary Gootie arrived a day early. My family were the first guests to register at the Camelot Motel, which officially opened for our celebration. The landscaping wasn't finished, and some of the rooms were unpainted. Construction workers mingled with returning fraternity members. To apologize for what the motel lacked, the Camelot management placed a bottle of champagne in every room. This gesture won

Gootie's heart. She immediately put the bottle in her food basket under the dry ice.

"I'll save it for your wedding," she said.

The celebration had little to do with me or any of the current members; we were just there because we had to be. As master of ceremonies I sat at the head table. I offered Terry a place beside me.

"No thanks," she said.

My parents also chose to sit less conspicuously. Since there was room, I placed Gootie and Rocky at the head table among all the past presidents since 1921. It seemed right. Gootie and Rocky were older than any of the alumni. I wanted Gootie to get special treatment for her first overnight trip in two generations. With Rocky close by I hoped I could keep him from calling the fraternity members "Odd Fellows."

I was glad to be occupied with all the details of the event; it gave me less time to worry about Gootie's meeting with Terry. My parents and Rocky would be meeting her for the first time, too, but the only opinion I worried about was Gootie's.

At the head table, Gootie drank soup from her own stainless-steel bowl. Rocky wore a yarmulke. They were as out of place at these events as they seemed to be. I heard Rocky call some of the old-timers "Odd Fellows," but I couldn't stop him. When I finished my speech I looked at Gootie. She was still eating her soup. Before the next speaker began Rocky left. He'd already heard what he came to hear.

Gootie had asked only a few relevant questions about Terry, and I gave the formulaic answers.

"Is she clean?"

"You can eat off her floors."

"Is it a good family?"

"Yes, no suicides, no divorces, Jews on all sides."

"Does she have whorish ways?"

"No," I said, "she tries to keep her elbows and knees covered."

"Who introduced you?"

"Nobody," I said. "I met her in the library."

"You don't just meet a girl," Gootie insisted. "Somebody always introduces. That's polite."

"I saw her lots of times. She studied near me. I noticed that when she studies she winds her legs around one another."

"Why?"

"Just a habit, the way some people bite their nails."

"Is she a Communist?"

"No, she loves President Kennedy. She worked for him in Chicago. She called people on the phone and asked them to vote for him."

"That's not a job," Gootie said. "Anybody can talk on the phone."

After dinner I led Gootie to a folding chair in the ballroom. Then I brought Terry over to introduce her. They were both wearing dark blue dresses. In heels and with her hair up Terry looked more slender than usual. Gootie sat not far from the band. She held a bottle of champagne, another gift that the motel manager had distributed, several to a table. All around us people who hadn't seen one another for decades were sharing photographs and exchanging life stories. Terry sat down and wound her legs.

"What should I say?" she whispered to me.

"Anything," I said.

"How do you like Ann Arbor?" Terry asked. I translated.

"A city is a city," Gootie said. "How's your health?"

"Okay, I guess," Terry said. "I have allergies, mostly hay fever. It's bad during the pollen season. I sneeze a lot."

"How many children, God willing, would you like?"

Terry hesitated. "I'm thinking of joining the Peace Corps."

Gootie looked to me for the explanation.

"She wants to help poor people," I said.

Gootie gestured toward the room. "They all look rich," she said.

"Not here," I said, "in other places all over the world."

"What are you going to do for them?" Gootie asked.

Terry rewound her legs. "I don't exactly know," she said. "Teach them things, I guess, about farming and hygiene."

One of the fraternity trustees called me away for a few minutes. When I returned Terry wasn't there and Gootie was directing Rocky to claim an unopened champagne bottle from one of the tables.

"Some hotel," Rocky said. "They give you champagne, but the television doesn't work."

"There's too much noise," Gootie said. "I'd rather go to the bedroom."

I led her through the crowd. She clutched her two champagne bottles.

"What did you think?" I asked her.

She waited until we had walked away from the noisy ballroom. "A lot of old people trying to act like they're young," she said. "Who do they think they're fooling?"

"The girl," I said. "What do you think of Terry?"

"I wasn't sure if she's the one you wanted me to meet."

"Of course she is. That's why I brought her over."

"What can I say? I talked to her for two minutes. If she's the one that's destined for you, that's what will be."

"Why didn't you talk to her longer?"

"I think she had to go to the bathroom," Gootie said. "She couldn't sit still."

"She was nervous."

"She might have TB. She told me she sneezes. Does she cough, too?"

"She doesn't have TB and you're not a doctor. I wanted you to meet her, not give her an examination."

"In Serei you wouldn't bring a girl like this to the wedding canopy. People would say, 'Fatten her up first. This isn't a wife; this is a board with a hole in it.'"

I went back to the celebration, where Terry waited for me.

"Sorry," she said, "I just couldn't talk to her. I don't think she understood me."

In the morning I walked Gootie to the car and thanked her for making the historic trip.

"Next time," she said, "I'll bet it will be the real one."

Chapter 29

While about a hundred tourists watched, Lili St. Cyr
disrobed. I couldn't see her face or her body. Steam surrounded
her. Yet the crowd cheered when she dropped her robe and
stepped into an oversize porcelain bathtub flowing with bubbles.

I had used my first complimentary coupon for lunch. My second
entitled me to watch Lili enjoy her daily bath.

I was in Las Vegas, on my way home from California, where I
was a graduate student. While Lili thrilled the crowd by raising
first one leg, then the other above the bubbles, I thought about a
different bather.

My mother, Bashy, tried not to alarm me. She didn't even call
to tell me what had happened until Gootie returned from the
hospital. "Dr. Farber says it wasn't a big stroke. You don't have to
hurry."

It took me four days to drive home. When I walked into her
room Gootie was sitting up in bed, propped up by her pillow.

"I'm okay," she said, "just a little weak."

"Lazy," Rocky added. "There's nothing wrong with her."

"Send him away. Tell him there's ten bags of flour for him to spoil at the bakery."

"Why did you come home?" Rocky asked. "Did you fail at school?"

"I just decided to take a rest."

"How can you rest when you don't do any work?"

"Don't answer him," Gootie advised. "Nobody's got the strength to talk to him."

She had wrapped a white rag around her head as if she had a headache, and there were smelling salts on her nightstand. "I'm tired of lying in bed," she said, "but it's too hard to do anything."

I held open a small paper bag and raised it to her eye level. "I've been saving all year, and I bought gas all the way back at places that give double and triple."

She reached her hand in and pulled out a few pages of Green Stamps. "When I'm a little stronger," she said, "we'll go look for a teakettle. The bottom of ours is wearing too thin. I should have bought copper the last time."

"We'll go to the bank, too," I said. "I'm taking time off from school. We'll be able to go wherever you want."

"Too late for the bank," she said. "I haven't been there in so long that they could have taken everything by now. I'll just have to trust them."

She tried to move her legs to the side of the bed but couldn't. "I don't know what happened to me," she said.

"You'll be all right."

"I'm tired of lying here looking out the window."

"I'll read to you. I brought a lot of books."

"Good," she said, "the books will make the day go by faster."

Through Gootie's bedroom window we could only see the backyard of her neighbor, Mrs. Witter, and no traffic moved along the narrow hallway outside her door. My sisters were married and lived in other states. Bashy delivered the meals and medicines. Rocky came in to rile her, but mostly Gootie and I had all day for reading. I had spent a year as a graduate student and no longer had any illusions about educating her.

Sometimes I read aloud in English; sometimes I translated directly to Yiddish. When I thought she was close to sleep I even read her *Beowulf* in Old English. She woke up to stop me.

"You sound like a dog barking," she said.

Her arms and legs were weak, but she hadn't lost her sense of plot. Although I read from books, Gootie treated every story as if I were making it up while I went along. She had never heard of Homer, but even in my translation she recognized a great story.

"She's a good-for-nothing," Gootie said about Helen of Troy, "and the king, what kind of a king runs after a woman for ten years? In ten years does he still think she'll be so beautiful? A smart man would forget about her and find a decent woman from a good family. That's better than being a king. With a good wife every man is a king."

I brought out all the books I had accumulated and stacked them against the wall in Gootie's room. While she slept I read to myself and filled her in on details. When we talked about Madame Bovary and Anna Karenina in the same week, Gootie stopped me.

"I don't want to hear any more," she said. "It's the same thing over and over. Don't you have any books about women who aren't whores?"

When we switched to Shakespeare, she didn't care for King Lear or his daughters, not even the good one. "She's as terrible as her sisters," Gootie said, "but she's smarter, so she pretends that she likes her father in case he's got more money hidden away some place. A man that rich always has more, and she knows she'll get it."

There were no Greeks in our Greek epics and no English in our English novels. We stayed close to home. The "wine-dark sea" became the Grand River, and the walls of Troy became the barbed-wire fence around the American Seating Company parking lot.

I told Gootie she was doing just what Shakespeare did—taking a story and changing it to suit herself. She didn't consider that a compliment.

"He was a crazy man," she said. "All he thought about was murderers and wars."

"He was the greatest writer ever," I said.

"I wouldn't give you a nickel for his books," Gootie said, but she didn't stop me from telling her more plots.

Our days were all similar. After her morning coffee, taken at around noon, I read and she listened or dozed. At three I carried lunch to her and at seven or eight her evening coffee. By nine she fell asleep for the night. On her most alert days she still worried about my future. I told her, almost before I admitted it to myself, that I was going to be a writer.

"Don't tell this to anyone else," she said. "We had a writer in Serei; his children lived in the poorhouse. He could write Yiddish and Russian and Polish, and everyone laughed at him. He had to put his face so close to the paper that people used to say he licked the ink off the page. His wife, poor soul, used to knock on doors asking people if they had any writing to be done."

"He probably needed glasses," I said. "If he had gone to an eye doctor he could have sat up straight and made a better living."

"If he had six eyes and four hands this man wouldn't have made a living. Finally after his wife died he stopped being a writer and he worked in a stable. He didn't make a living there, either."

"In America it's different," I told her. "Anyway, I'm not going to copy things for people. I'm going to write stories that I make up."

"If you go around saying that," she said, "people will talk about you behind your back. They'll say, 'There goes Mr. Pencil-and-Paper.' Then you really won't find anyone to marry."

"You're wrong," I said. "Girls like to talk about stories just like you do."

"When I was young I didn't talk about stories," she said. "If I told my father I wanted to marry a man who made up stories, he would have cut his jacket and sat shivah. A person who makes up stories is a swindler. The prisons are full of them."

One day she surprised me. "If you're such a writer," Gootie said, "read me one of your stories instead of all this 'She kissed him when her husband went to work.'"

I had one that I thought she'd like.

"No whores," she said.

"None—and there's even someone you know, your nephew Phil."

"Yachey's son, Phil?" she asked. "Then tell me. He deserves to be in a story; he's such an operator."

He was an operator in that story, a wrestling promoter—his chief attraction, a powerful female wrestler named "Terry" who dressed in tiger-skin tights and threw her opponents over the ropes.

Gootie laughed. "Nobody will believe you," she said. "She's too skinny to pick up a person."

"It's not the Terry you're thinking of," I said. "I just used the same name."

"There are so many names in the world, why did you pick hers?"

"Because I think of her sometimes," I admitted. "I like the name."

"Pick another one," she said, "a livelier name."

I renamed the wrestler "Harriet."

"Better," Gootie said. "Keep Phil the way he is—he's good. But the girl, don't make her a wrestler. Why should she be a crazy person?"

"She has to be a wrestler," I said. "The whole story is about wrestling."

"So change it," she said.

I left the written story the way it was, but for Gootie I made Harriet a housewife who married a salesman. They had three children. One day her husband came home from the synagogue and told her he had taken up with another woman, a young widow. He hadn't slept with her—she was an honorable woman—but when he looked at the widow, he thought to himself, I'm married to the wrong person.

He and the widow prayed for forgiveness. They fasted; they visited rabbis and holy men.

"This is a real story," Gootie said. "What did the rabbis say?"

"The rabbis told him he should have realized sooner what he wanted in a wife. 'You don't marry a Leah and expect a Rachel,' they said."

"They're exactly right," Gootie said, "and when you get married it should be forever, not changing wives and husbands every Monday and Thursday like they do in America."

"That's what the rabbis said, all of them," I told her.

"I know what I'm talking about," she said.

A few weeks later Gootie returned to the hospital. I brought her big pillow to St. Mary's. It got in the nurses' way, but nobody told me to take it home. She slept most of the time, and when she woke I told her more stories. One day I read her one that I knew she'd like by Chekhov, a Russian.

"He might have been in Odessa while you were," I said, "who knows? He wrote a story about gooseberries."

"Americans don't even know what they are. We had them," she said. "Do you remember?"

I remembered. I told her Chekhov's story about a man who gave up everything so he could have an estate and grow his own gooseberries.

"He married a rich woman, but he didn't love her."

"How rich?" Gootie asked.

"Her husband was a postmaster."

"Not so rich," she said.

"He took her money and he didn't give her enough to eat, just black bread once a day. After she died he bought a farm and planted twenty gooseberry bushes. He acted like a big shot; he made all the workers call him 'sir.' Finally he got his gooseberries, fat green ones from all twenty bushes. He ordered his servant to bring him bowls full and he stuffed himself. 'This is the life,' he said, 'my own gooseberries.'"

"In Serei," Gootie said, "lots of people had gooseberries and without starving their wives to get them. You remember—you were only a little boy, but you remember what went on there."

When she mistook me for her son I didn't correct her, and I didn't even think she was wrong. The generation that I missed, she filled me in on. The village that I never saw, she peopled for me.

While Gootie slept through most of her days in St. Mary's Hospital, I sat at the desk in her room and began to write stories about Serei. I knew the place as well as I knew Grand Rapids. I imagined her and her brothers Joe and Louie before they ran off to make their fortunes in America. I wrote about Leo and Yachey, not Alma millionaires, a peddler and his young wife, taking in boarders for a few extra dollars a week.

Like Gootie, I didn't settle for the old stories; I added new people and events—an American Indian and a Russian general, and I wrote about the Russo-Japanese War, which Joe just missed, and about Gootie's parents, Beryl Leib and Rachel Leah, who couldn't imagine a place like America where Jews lived just like everyone else.

Sometimes Gootie opened her eyes. When she did that I imagined her climbing the mountain the way Moses did to look at the future. Gootie couldn't climb as high or see as much. She didn't look beyond Serei and Grand Rapids. Even with all the world spread before her, the greatest attraction lay behind the hedges that she planted herself to give privacy to her gooseberries, her currants, and her grandchildren.

Sometimes a nurse or a sister or an orderly stayed in the room for an extra minute to listen as I read. One of the sisters held Gootie's hand.

"She must have been a great reader."

"Not really," I said, "but she likes stories."

"Then you keep on reading," the St. Mary's sister said. "Somebody's listening. I'm sure of that."

I never doubted it.

When Gootie checked into the next world's version of the Pantlind Hotel, she left me the two bottles of champagne she had been saving for my wedding. They evaporated, but nothing else has faded. Her down and feathers cover her great-grandchildren, who sometimes sneeze from the dust accumulated by their ancestors.

She left me her husband, who lasted into the next generation, and she left me two stores after all—her Serei and her America. The older I get, the less I can tell them apart. They're both full of the best bargains—real characters—people you can laugh at and still learn something from.

She left my sisters her women's prayer books, but I received my share of the God they tell about, as busy as ever making matches.

She left me her sense of loss and the will to live beyond it. And she left me her recipe for stories. You start with a good person and you see what happens next. You listen and you watch. By the end it all adds up to something.